INTRODUCTION
TO
THE VEDAS

By

Dr. Ravi Prakash Arya

Amazon Books, USA
in association with
Indian Foundation for Vedic Science
1051, Sector-1, Rohtak, Haryana, India Pin124001
Ph. No. 09313033917; 09650183260
Email : vedicscience@gmail.com; vedicscience@rediffmail.com
web: www.vedicscience.net

First Edition

Kali era: 5119 (c. 2017)
Kalpa era: 1,97,29,49,119
Brahma era: 15,55,21,97,29,49,119

ISBN 81- 87710-41-1

Contents

Preface

Dear readers! Let me inform you that this treatise a compilation and collection of lectures delivered by the author of present lines to the online participants of the course on 'Introduction to the Vedas' run by the Indian Foundation for Vedic Science. In the present compilation, a humble attempt has been made to introduce readers to the Vedas and their various components. Hope it will enable our readers to understand the Vedas and Indian Intellectual tradition in the right earnest.

This treatise will also help you to understand various aspects and terms pertaining to the Vedas, the Vedic life, and thought correctly and open up new vistas of research. It will also help you enhance your interest in this oldest literature of humankind on the globe. Here an effort has been made to present Vedic Mantras in original form through Devanāgarī font, although their Roman transliteration has also been provided for those who are unable to read Hindi or Sanskrit. Hope our readers will find this work very helpful to brush up their knowledge on the most ancient literature of the world.

Dr. Ravi Prakash Arya

Introductory Note

When we talk about the Veda, we, generally, have a picture of holy scriptures in mind. We generally think that the Vedas are the same category of literature as that of the Bible or the Quran. People think that the Vedas are related to the Hindus as the Bible and the Quran to the Christians and the Muslims respectively. In fact, this view received its first sanction at the hands of various European scholars who started the studies of the Vedas having regarded them as religious scriptures of the Hindus. This was evident from Max Müller's series called by him as the '*The Sacred Books of the East Series*'. That is why the Vedas were also categorised in the list of sectarian or communal literature. The Vedas, in fact, are the documents dealing with God's creation. They exist since the time humanity came into existence on this globe. By then, there was no religion or sect on the earth. The Vedas were regarded as sacred, not because that they were related to a particular community or because they were composed by the prophet of a particular community, but because they were the storehouse of all the true sciences; because they represented the various aspects of creation and cosmic life; because they contained the universal laws irrespective of caste, creed, race, religion or region.

If we want to understand the Vedas in the true sense, we must have a clear view of the three entities which are interwoven, interlinked, and complement each other. These three entities are:

1. The Yajña

2. The Veda

3. The Itihāsa & Purāṇa

Briefly, we must know that the Yajña refers to the process of creation of living and non-living world right from the origin of matter, energy, and space. The Veda refers to the blueprint/knowledge of creation. The Itihāsa & Purāṇa refer to the history of creation. Thus the origin and development of the entire Indian Intellectual tradition revolve around the Yajña, i.e. creation of the universe. The Vedas originated to define this creation and Itihāsa & Purāṇa came into being to record the history of creation. Itihāsa and Purāṇas were used as illustrations while elucidating the Vedas. That is why it has repeatedly been pronounced in the Vedic tradition that the Vedas can better be elucidated and explained with the help of Itihāsa and Purāṇa- इतिहासपुराणाभ्यां वेदं समुपबृंहयेत् – *Itihāsa-purāṇābhyāṁ vedaṁ sam upabṛṁhayet.* Now we would like to touch different aspects from the point of their importance. Hope our readers will enjoy this oldest treasure of humanity.

What is Veda?

The word 'Veda' is derived from the root √vid, meaning to know. So the Veda means knowledge.

The Vedas, as the blueprint of creation, represent its various aspects -metaphysical, astrophysical, and physical aspects. Since the creation of the universe is the handiwork of God, the authorship of creation can be assigned to God alone and none else. So, the authorship of knowledge of creation contained in the Vedas is assigned to almighty God. As such the Vedas are called *apauruṣeyas.*

Origin and Authorship of the Vedas

There has long been a debate as to whether the Vedas were authored by God or man. It has always been answered: वेदाः अपौरुषेयाः – *vedāḥ apauruṣeyāḥ*, i.e. the Vedas are not authored by Puruṣa (man). The term Puruṣa has been used to signify both man and God by the various contenders in order to support their contentions. It must be understood that the term Puruṣa here does not mean God but man. So the term वेदाः अपौरुषेयाः '*vedāḥ apauruṣeyāḥ*' would only mean 'the Vedic knowledge is not the man-made knowledge'.

The other way round also, the Veda, as pointed out above, being knowledge, or dharma would reside permanently in its dharmī, the object, i.e. Brahman who is All-knowing, whilst a man knows a little. Brahman alone is qualified by knowledge of creation being its sole creator. The knowledge is the inherent quality of God.

Moreover, it can again be proved on the evidence gathered from the Vedic literature. For example, the *Śatapatha Brāhmaṇa* (14.5.4.10) has made a clear cut statement that the Vedas are the expressions of creation. Accordingly:

एवं वा अरेऽस्यमहतो भूतस्य निःश्वसितम्।
एतद्यदृग्वेदो यजुर्वेदः सामवेदोऽथर्वागिंरसः।।

evam vaa are'sya mahato bhūtasya niḥśvasitam.
etad-vā Ṛgvedo Yajurvedaḥ Sāmavedo'tharvāṅgirasaḥ.

[Meaning] The couplets that are known as the *Ṛgveda*, the *Yajurveda*, the *Sāmveda,* and the *Atharvaveda* are the exhalations (blueprint) of this grand creation.

At another place in the same work, it has been clearly picturised leaving no space for further doubt and suspense regarding the God made the Vedas. According to the *Śatpatha Brāhmaṇa* (11.5.4.17):

द्वय्यो वा इमाः प्रजाः दैव्यश्चैव मानुष्यश्च। ता वा इमा मानुष्यः प्रजाः प्रजननात्प्रजायन्ते। छन्दांसि वै दैव्यः प्रजाः। तानि मुखतो जनयते, तत् एतं जनयते।

'There are two types of creations. One is man-made produced through the sexual behaviour. Another is divine or God-made cosmic-creation. Chhandas (metrical couplets of the Vedas) are God made creation, as they came into being with the cosmic creation. They are produced by Ṛṣis through their mouth. Instead of sexual intercourse'.

Thus from the foregoing discussion, it can

unhesitatingly be inferred that the couplets of the Vedas or Chhandas present in the cosmos received/imbibed by Brahmā in Samādhi at the beginning of creation were the literary items originated first ever in the literary history of humankind. These chhandas that were the blueprint of the cosmic creation of God or say authored by God were pronounced by the Ṛṣis through their mouth.

Here Gitā's view on the Veda may also be quoted. Gīta (2.45) says, त्रिगुण्यविषया वेदाः– *triguṇya vıṣayā vedāḥ*, i.e. the Vedas deal with the *triguṇātmaka prakṛti.* The material creation evolved out of the imbalance of three guṇas, viz. sattva, rajas, and tamas.

The above-cited view and the Gīta on the Vedas clearly point out that the Vedas are the knowledge of creation and the creation is the handy work of the almighty God. As such the authorship of the Vedas, the knowledge of creation can be assigned to God alone and not to any human being propounding it. For example, an engineer who creates an engine becomes the author of the knowledge of the engine. When a potter makes a pot, he becomes the author of the pot. Similarly, when Brahman creates the universe, He becomes the author of His creation and so also the author of the Vedas. This process may also be illustrated by the following example.

Whenever anything is created its knowledge comes into existence in the cosmos immediately after its creation. Similarly, when God created this universe, His knowledge of the creation of the universe, i.e Veda came into existence in the cosmos immediately after the origin of creation took place. Brahmā had a direct insight of this universal knowledge called the Veda in his Samādhi. This process of direct insight is also called enlightenment or revelation. Patañjali, the author of the *Yoga Darśana* (1.47) has shed an ample good light on this process of direct insight.

निर्विचारवैशारद्येऽध्यात्मप्रसादः ।

nirvichāra-vaiśāradye adhyātmaprasadaḥ

According to him, when a high profile Yogī attains perfection in nir-vichāra Samādhi (a state of mind in which a Yogī can meditate even without contents), his intellect becomes free from rajas and tamas guṇas and settles down permanently in sattva guṇa and clears off all thoughts. At this stage, his intellect transforms into 'prajñā' which is the highest form of intellect.

ऋतम्भरा तत्र प्रज्ञा

ṛtambharā tatra prajñā (*Yoga Darśana,* 1.48)

Here 'prajñā' bears the 'ṛta' (cosmic laws) directly. When a person rises to the state of prajñā, he knows truth directly without the intermediary of language or thought. He achieves a state of direct enlightenment. His knowledge then is perfect. What he sees is the truth, because it is directly realised and free of subjective and situational conditions and the limitations of thought and language. His knowledge is not relative now. It is absolute which is nothing else but the Vedas. This is how Brahmā had direct access to the knowledge of creation through his prajñā at the beginning of human creation. In fact, this creation is the embodiment of the Vedas. It is the vāk (speech) of Brahman. Since this creation is exclusive work of Brahman, so it is verily said, एको वेदः – *eko vedaḥ* (the Veda is one). This Veda exists in two forms:

1. In the visible form as a universe.

2. In the audible form as vibrations or quanta.

Thus everybody sees this Veda of creation, but very few except Brahmā are capable of reading and comprehending it. Everybody is not able to hear this speech. That is why in the Ṛgveda (10.71.4), it is said:

उत त्वः पश्यन्न ददर्श वाचमुत त्वः शृण्वन्न शृणोत्येनाम्।
उतो त्वस्मै तन्वं१ वि सस्रे जायेव पत्य उशती सुवासाः।।

uta tvaḥ paśyanna dadarśa vācham

uta tvaḥ śṛṇvanna śṛṇotyenām
uto tvasmai tanvaṁ visasre
jāyeva patya uśatī suvāsā

There are some who on seeing the Veda (speech) in the form of creation does not see (understand) it, while another hearing the speech (vibrations/quanta of the universe) does not hear it. The Veda unfolds itself to the deserving seer like the wife to her husband.

In other words, it can be said that creation is the manifestation of the Veda (natural laws) and the Veda is the expression of creation. Thus they are mutually inter-dependant. The 'ṛta' or natural laws remain the same at all levels of nature and the universe, while their expression as we know is quite varied. The underlying laws (ṛta and satya) are the same even when they express themselves in different forms, shapes, components, and levels of sophistication, complexity, and completeness. The Veda has expressly disclosed this fact, as

एकं सद् विप्रा बहुधा वदन्ति।

ekam sad viprā bhudhā vadanti

There is only one underlying law or truth expressed in different forms.

In its most abstract form, the underlying law and truth is nothing but the will of Brahman that creates and organises the whole physical or biological universe. Human life and the world are also governed by it. This will of Brahman, in his true sense, can also be appreciated through mathematical formulae, laws of physics, chemistry, biology, anatomy, or physiology, but can also be understood in terms of family, social and national structures. The manifestation of unified law in various forms takes place due to the factor of māyā. इन्द्रो मायाभिः पुरुरूप ईयते। If one is able to transcend this māyā factor in the universe, known variously as the 'unified law' or the 'will of Brahman' or the 'Veda', will unfold itself to him. This unified law is the subject of subjective experience and its manifestation into various forms of the universe is the subject of objective assessment. It exists in the objectively assessed physical universe as a 'unified field', but on the subjective level of experience, it unfolds itself as Brahman (pure consciousness, self-referral soul (pure Being), and ultimate truth. So the unified field and unified law are the two sides of the same coin. In the context of subjective internal experience, it is the 'unified law', but in the context of the objective external universe, it is a 'unified field' in its abstract form.

What is māyā? Prakṛti is the unified state of sattva (intelligence), rajas (energy), and tamas (inertia). When this unification is disturbed spontaneously (known as the will of Brahman), the vikṛti starts taking place. This spontaneous disturbance in unification takes place due to the principle of māyā at work. Māyā is a spiritual concept connoting "that which exists, but is constantly changing and thus is spiritually unreal", and the "power or the principle that conceals the true character of spiritual reality". So the principle of māyā is the principle of change. This principle of māyā is at work in all spheres of life. In day to day life when we become bored and tired of the routine life, we want a change, it is also because of the principle of māyā or the law of change known as the principle law of nature. It may also be termed as dynamism. This māyā or dynamism exists in the very nature of Brahman. He does not want to be static, rather as dynamic He is, He wants the change of state. This want of a change of state by Brahman has been expressed in several Vedic statements like एकोऽहं बहु स्याम – *eko'ham bahu syām*, etc. This desire for change comes spontaneously in Brahman without any condition, situational, or subjective whatsoever. Nature and we all have inherited this habit of change from the Brahman Himself. So natural law or will of God is one and the same thing. It is called natural law from an objective perspective, but the same is called the Will of Brahman (God) from a spiritual or subjective angle or consideration. Natural law is also known as the law of divine or divine law. Coming back to the same point, it can be observed that in the state of prakṛti, all-natural forces were also unified into one fundamental force. However, during the state of vikṛti due to the principle of māyā, the grand unification of forces also disintegrates and they start separating and manifest into various forms undergoing to various phases of change till the atoms are formed and come together to make molecules, molecules collecting to create cells, and groups of cells forming tissues and organs and organisms.

Now the question arises as to what makes atoms, molecules, and cells come together as they do? The answer is the principle of māyā or say the law of change of nature or law of dynamism of nature. The change of state takes place by permutations and combinations of various components. Although at the different change of phases, there seem to be different laws at work, but they all express the same unified law of māyā which permeates them all and which remains unchanged, which is the source of all forces, energy and particles and a field of pure existence. This unified law contains the details of all natural laws in the seed form. Theoretician physicists and mathematicians try to describe them through their formulae and equations. The universe thus is the cosmic shape of Prakṛti (potential energy). Just as a seed contains the tree in pure potentiality; the tree is the manifest shape of inner hidden dynamics available in seed, similarly, Prakṛti contains the universe in pure potentiality and the universe is the manifest shape of inner dynamics (sattva/intelligence, rajas/energy, and tamas/inertia) available in prakṛti. Thus prakṛti is the seed of the universe which grows into a universe following an orderly process of creation (ṛta) from the creator with goals and intentions. So, at one level (unified level/unmanifest level), natural law is pure prakṛti (unified state of sattva/intelligence, rajas/energy, and tamas/inertia; on another (diversified level/manifest level) it is particles and matter; then it is unicellular and multicellular organisms.

The prakṛti or natural law manifests itself in a hierarchy of forms or expressions which are as under:

1. **Mahat**: The first manifestation of prakṛti takes place in the form of mahat. Mahat is universal or collective intelligence. So the first phase of the evolution of the universe takes place with the origin of the collective intelligence of the universe. Mahat can be divided into three parts sāttvika mahat (pure collective intelligence of the universe), rājasika mahat (collective energy of the universe which is a mix of intelligence and matter), and tāmasika mahat (pure collective inertia of the universe).

2. **Ahaṅkāra**: Mahat (collectiveness) expresses/ transforms itself into ahaṅkāra, i.e. into discreteness (individually separate and distinct identity). Ahaṅkāra is discreteness. As such sāttvika mahat (pure collective intelligence of the universe) transforms into sāttvika ahaṅkāra (discrete or individually separate distinct units of intelligence in the universe called souls accompanied by a subtle body consisting of mind and intellect often known as individual consciousness). Rājasika mahat (collective energy of the universe) transforms itself into rājasika ahaṅkāra (discrete units of energy in the universe or energy particles/massless particles) and tāmasika mahat (collective inertia of the universe) transforms itself into tāmasika ahaṅkāra (discrete units of inertia or matter particles/particles with mass).

Yāska (*Nirukta*, 1.20) while narrating the history of the origin of the Vedas says, 'There were Ṛṣis who had a direct insight of Dharma (laws of creation in the form of the Veda Mantras or chhandas). This knowledge was passed on through oral instructions to succeeding generations of Ṛṣis who were devoid of powers of direct insight. They further passed this knowledge on to their successors in documented form who failed to receive it through oral instructions.'

Thus Brahmā was the first Ṛṣi who had the direct

insight of the Vedas, the blueprint of creation. He categorised this knowledge as the *Ṛgveda*, the *Yajurveda*, the *Sāmaveda,* and the *Atharvaveda* and passed to the four Ṛṣis, namely Agni, Vāyu, Āditya, and Aṅgirā. The classification of the Vedas (the knowledge of the creation of living and non-living world) into the *Ṛgveda*, the *Yajurveda*, the Sāmaveda, and the Atharvaveda will be discussed in ensuing chapters. Presently, it suffices to understand that four-fold the Vedas deal with various aspects of the creation.

The *Ṛgveda* deals with all the components of creation viz. metaphysical, astrophysical, and physical.

The *Yajurveda* deals with the process of the creation. This process of the creation is called as Yajña, particularly Śrauta Yajña. The various phases of creation have been depicted by various types of Śrauta Yajñas.

The *Sāmaveda* deals with the cosmic vibrations called as Sāma Gānas. The entire universe is buzzing with sounds/vibrations which are not audible to the ordinary human ears. Only the high profile yogī-s can enjoy these divine sounds.

The *Atharvaveda* deals with all aspects of the mundane life. This material creation would have become meaningless, had there been no biological life. In fact, the presence of living beings gives meaning to this material creation. So the very objective of the *Atharvaveda* is to deal with the origin and evolution of biological life, particularly the life of human beings.

Based upon the foregoing discussion, it can unhesitatingly be said that the Vedas are nothing but the science of creation, representing all its three aspects, i.e. adhibhautika (physical or geophysical), adhidaivika (astronomical or astrophysical), and adhyātmika (metaphysical or spiritual). Thus in more vivid and lucid terms, it can be stated that the Vedas are a science:

(1). That defines the relationship between mind, body, and soul at the adhyātmika or metaphysical level.

(2). That defines the phenomena of life and death.

(3). That defines the relationship between the biological life and the physical life in the context of the earth and the cosmos beyond.

(4). That defines the relationship between the living body and the cosmic body.

(5). That defines the parallelism between physical, astronomical, and metaphysical levels of creation. In other words, it defines the relationship between physics, astrophysics, and metaphysics.

To sum up it can be stated that the Vedas are a science of the earth, a science of the cosmos, and a science of spirituality or consciousness.

Documentation of the Vedas

The Vedas, as already informed, are the blueprint of the creation of the living and non-living world. This blueprint existed in the cosmos since creation. It was perceived directly by the high-spirited yogī-s coded in the form of the Vedas. The process of creation of living and the non-living beings is known as first operation/Yajña, whereas the documentation of the blueprint of this Yajña of creation is called the second operation/Yajña. When the first operation/ Yajña (creation) was over the Devas (High-spirited yogī-s) performed the second operation/Yajña (documentation of the laws governing the creation of the living and non-living world). This fact is confirmed by the Vedas as follows.

> 'The Divine beings like Brahmā and other seers visualised the blueprint of creation (Yajña) that physically existed before them. This visualisation was the first Dharma (unified law of creation). These laws of creation speak highly of light space (nāka) which is the source of this creation[1].'

In fact, all laws of creation visualised by the seers were coded in the forms of literary couplets or Chhandas. Those couplets or Chhandas were regarded as Dharmas, the laws governing the creation. This is why, Yāska (*Nirukta*, 1.20), an ancient Indian Vedic scholar alludes to the Origin of the

---

1 यज्ञेन यज्ञमयजन्त देवाः तानि धर्माणि प्रथमान्यासन्।
ते ह नाकं महिमानः सचन्त यत्र पूर्वे साध्या सन्ति देवाः।।
yajñena yajñam-ayajanta
devās-tāni dharmāṇi-prathamānyāsana
te ha nākam mahimānaḥ sacanta
yatra pūrve sādhyāḥ santi devāḥ.

(The *Ṛgveda*, 1.164.50; 10.90.16; the *Atharvaveda*, 7.5.1; the *Vājasaneyī Saṁhitā*, 31.16; the *Taittirīya Saṁhitā*, 3.5.11.5; the *Taittirīya Āraṇyaka*, 3.2.7)

Vedas (Chhandas) as:

> 'There were ṛṣis to whom was revealed Dharma (unified law governing creation coded in the form of the Veda Mantras or Chhandas). They taught this dharma to their followers who were devoid of it, through oral instructions. When the later generation of Ṛṣis was not able to retain this knowledge through oral instructions, all these laws were subjected to documentation just to aid them[2].

The records of the Vedas also tell us that on the basis of first operation/Yajña (creation) which occurred on account of oblations of all kinds of particles or forces, the origin of ṛcas contained in the *Ṛgveda*, sāmans contained in the *Sāmaveda*, yajuṣas contained in the *Yajurveda* and other Chhandas contained in the *Atharvaveda* took place in the cosmos. One of the seers of the *Vājasaneyī Saṁhitā* (31.7) sheds an ample good light on this fact as:

> 'From the Yajña (creation), in which oblations of all particles and forces were made, originated Ṛcas, Sāmans, Yajuṣas and other Chhandas (the *Atharvaveda*)[3].'

In fact, in that cosmic Yajña of creation, no material oblation was offered, as usual. However, ṛcas acted as the oblations of milk. Similarly, yajuṣas acted as oblations of Ghee, and the sāmans acted as the oblations of the Soma. This fact has been very carefully disclosed in the *Śatapatha Brāhmaṇa* (11.5.6.3,4,5)[4]. Here it may be pointed out that the sage to whom the knowledge of creation was revealed was Brahmā who passed this knowledge on to four ṛṣis,

---

2 *sākṣāt-kṛt-dharmāṇaḥ ṛṣayoḥ babhūvuḥ.*

3 *tasmād yajñātsarvahutaḥ ṛcaḥ sāmāni jajñire.*
chandāṁsi jajñire tasmād yajus-tasmādajāyata.

4 *paya āhutayo ha vā etā devānāṁ yad ṛcaḥ*
ājyāhutayo ha vā etā devānāṁ yad yajuṁṣi.
somāhutayo ha vā etā devāmāṁ yat sāmāni.

viz. Agni, Vāyu, Āditya, and Aṅgirā.

Classification of literary Couplets, or Chhandas into Ṛk, Yajuḥ, and Sāman

As a result of the second great operation/Yajña (documentation of revealed knowledge in coded form) by the enlightened ṛṣi Brahmā, a huge number of couplets/Chhandas came into being dealing with mass-energy existing at various levels of creation, viz. Bhumi (earth or observer space), dyau (the sun or light space), and field or Intervening space between Bhumi and Dyau. For example,

1. Agni as geothermal energy in the earth and as mass-energy of observer space.

2. Field energy or Vāyu in the space intervening earth and sun.

3. Sūrya as the light of the sun (star) and as the mass-energy of the light space.

Thus the knowledge received about the geothermal energy of earth or mass-energy of light space called (Agni) and its sub-forms was coded as ṛcā. The knowledge received about field energy (Vāyu), and electric force (Indra) and their forms existing in the space intervening earth and the sun was coded as yajuṣas and the knowledge of the sunrays and mass-energy of light space and its sub-forms was coded as sāmans. The *Śvetāśvatara Upanıṣada* (6.18), the *Aitareya Brāhmaṇa* (25.7) and the *Manusmṛti* (1.23) had it as:

> 'To make the second great operation/Yajña a success, three types of (brahmas) Vedic couplets were derived. From Agni (geothermal energy of the earth and mass-energy of observer space) were derived ṛcas; from Vāyu (field energy of space intervening earth and sun, or the observer space and the light space) were derived yajuṣas and from Sūrya (light of the sun or mass-energy of light space) were

derived sāmans[5].

N.B.: Here Brahma means 'Veda' that is why Brahmacārī is always known who undertakes the study of the Veda.

According to the *Śatapatha Brāhmaṇa* (11.5.8.3)

'On account of three forms of energy (tapta) in three spaces, three of the Vedas came into being. On account of Agni (geothermal energy of the earth and mass-energy of observer space) came into being; couplets called ṛcas or the *Ṛgveda*, on account of Vāyu (field energy or electric force of space intervening earth and sun; observer space and light space) came into being; yajuṣas or the *Yajurveda* and on account of Sūrya (light of the sun or mass-energy of light space) came into being the *Sāmaveda* or sāmans[6].'

The emergence of Saṁhitā literature

Later on, couplets dealing with ṛcas, yajusas, sāmans, and other chhandas were consolidated and compiled ṛṣi-wise and deity-wise into different literary styles and classified as the *Ṛk Saṁhitā,* the *Yājuṣa-Saṁhitā*, and the *Sāma Saṁhitā* respectively regardless of their earlier classification. During the course of the new classification, knowledge coded in metrical style was compiled as the *Ṛk Saṁhitā* (*ṛgarcanī*). Knowledge coded in prose style was separately compiled in the name of the *Yājuṣa Saṁhitā* (*yat praślıṣṭaṁ paṭhitaṁ tat yajuḥ*) and the knowledge coded to the tune of cosmic vibrations was compiled under the caption the *Sāma Saṁhitā.* (*gitıṣu sāmākhyā*). The knowledge of miscellaneous nature coded metrically was

---

5 *agni vāyu-ravibhyastu trayam brahma sanātanam*
dudoha yajña siddyarathaṁ ṛg-yajuḥ-sāma-lakṣaṇam

6 *tebhyas-taptebhyas-trayo vedā ajāyanta*
agner-ṛgvedo vāyor yajur vedaḥ sūryāt-sāmavedaḥ

compiled under the title *Atharva Saṁhitā*. So the *Atharva Saṁhitā* became the representative of all other three *Saṁhitās*. This will be elaborated in the next chapter.

Components of the Vedas

The four the Vedas have four components

1. Mantra
2. Ṛṣi
3. Devatā
4. Chhanda and
5. Svara

Mantra

The Mantra is a visualisation of a seer. Yāska (Kali era 2000-2100 or c.10th-11th century BC), an ancient Vedic scholar, defines Mantra as *mantrāḥ mananāt*, i.e. Mantra is revelation or visualisation of a reality or a truth. The word Mantra is formed of a root √man 'to know' 'to realise' 'to be enlightened'. The Mantra is the realisation of truth or reality or enlightenment. All the four the Vedas are composed of Mantras. These Mantras can be categorised into three types as per their literary style.

The Ṛk Mantras

The Yājus Mantras and

The Sāma Mantras

A Mantra coded in a metrical style called Ṛk. The *Ṛgveda* is a collection of 10589 ṛchā-s (Mantras) used for appreciating the properties of various forces instrumental in creation. It is said: *ṛgarcani,* i.e ṛcā-s were used for appreciation.

The Yajus Mantras were coded in prose style. It is said: *yat praślıṣṭaṁ paṭhitaṁ tat yajuḥ i.e.* Yajus Mantras are read like prose. The *Yajurveda Saṁhitā* is a collection of 1975 Mantras used in allegorical rituals (Śrauta Yajñas) representing some or other aspect of the process of creation taking place in our Universe. It includes all the Yajus

Mantras and some Ṛk Mantras from the *Ṛgveda.*

The Sāma Mantras were coded to the tune of cosmic vibrations and sung in musical style. It is said: *gitiṣu sāmākhyā* i.e. sāma is used for singing cosmic songs. *Sāma Saṁhitā* is a collection of 1875 Mantras representing various cosmic vibrations. They include all the Sāma Mantras and some Ṛk Mantras.

The *Atharva Saṁhitā* consists mainly of Ṛks and some Yajuṣas. The *Atharvaveda* has a collection of 5989 Mantras. There are roughly 1200 Ṛks and 600 Yajuṣas in the *Atharvaveda.* There are several Mantras common to the *Ṛgveda,* the *Yajurveda,* and the *Atharvaveda.* These all Mantras deal with different aspects of the mundane life.

The Mantras of the *Ṛk Saṁhitā,* the *Yājuṣa-Saṁhitā,* and the *Sāma Saṁhitā* are pronounced differently. The Mantras of the *Ṛk Saṁhitā* are chanted metrically. The Mantras of the *Yājuṣa-Saṁhitā* are chanted in a prose style and the Mantras of the *Sāma Saṁhitā* are chanted musically. The same Mantra if happens to be in the *Ṛgveda* is chanted as a Ṛk, if it occurs in the *Yajurveda* is chanted as a Yājuṣ text and if it occurs in the *Sāmaveda* is chanted as a Sāma Mantra.

Ṛṣi

Ṛṣi or seer is a yogī who is capable of visualising the truth or reality directly from the cosmos by supra-sensual hearing or sight. The cosmos is a laboratory of Brahman where all experiments are going on. A seer is able to see all these experiments by his supra-sensual sight. He is different from a scientist. A scientist has no access to the cosmic laboratory but he tries to know the reality by repeating the same in the lab. On the other hand, a yogī is able to see the things happening actually in the cosmos and describe them in a coded language. Thus the experience of a yogī is first hand, whereas that of a scientist is second hand. Each Mantra of the Veda has a Ṛṣi and Devatā associated with it. Ṛṣis are supposed to have visualised or received the Mantra. Yāska (2.11) describes Ṛṣi as one who has seen the Mantra[7] In this sense, Brahmā is a ṛṣi who saw the Mantras at the beginning of human creation on the earth. He handed down these Mantras to his four successors. The ṛk Mantras were handed over to Agni, the yājuṣ Mantras to Vāyu, the sāma Mantras to Aditya, and the atharva Mantras to Aṅgiras. As such in the beginning, the name of ṛṣis was well known and it could not then have been necessary to compile *Āıṣānukramaṇis* (Index of Ṛṣis) and the *Sarvānukramaṇis* (Index of Ṛṣis, Devata and Chhanda associated to the Mantras) like that of Kātyāyana, the author of the *Sarvānukramaṇi.* But when this tradition of the Mantras used to be handed down to ṛṣis in succession for millennia together, these Mantras became a legacy of more than 800 ṛṣis who inherited them in tradition. Later they were known as the inheritors of the Mantras preserved by them and their names were also associated with those Mantras. In this connection, Kātyāyana describes a ṛṣi is one whose utterance it is.[8] Saṁvād Sūktas (Dialogue Hymns) of the Vedas present several natural forces in a conversational mode, i.e they have been shown as if talking to each other. The example is the Ṛgvedic Yama-Yamī Sūkta. In these hymns, the speaker is known as Ṛṣi and the subject of his speech is known as Devatā. Here it may also be informed that several Ṛṣis became known by the names of fundamental particles or forces described in the Mantras inherited by them. As such these Ṛṣis associated with various Mantras are not the actual seers of the Mantras but they are their inheritors who were able to explain their intended sense as per context. Since the number of these Ṛṣis was excessive, it was not possible to remember them by the Vedic students, so the compilation of Ārṣānukramaṇis (Index of Ṛṣis) and Sarvānukramaṇis (Index of Ṛṣis, Devatā-s and Chhandas associated to Mantras) came into being. There are 330 Ṛṣis associated

---

7. *ṛṣayoḥ vai mantra-draṣṭāraḥ*

8. *yasya vākyaṁ sa ṛṣī*

with the *Ṛgveda* Mantras, 168 Ṛṣis associated with the *Yajurveda* Mantras, 217 Ṛṣis associated with the *Sāmaveda* Mantras and 76 Ṛṣis associated to the *Atharvaveda.*

Devatā (Deity)

Devatā or deity is the scientific truth revealed in the *Mantra.* In other words, the subject matter of the Mantra is known as Devatā.[9] Each Mantra has its Devatā. The word Devatā is an extended form of the word Deva. It is said:

देव एव देवता *Deva eva Devata,* i.e. any spiritual, natural force is Deva. Yāska (Kali era 2000-2100 or c 10th-11th century BC) defines Deva as:

देवो कस्मात्। दानाद्वा द्योतनाद्वा द्युस्थानो भवतीति वा

Devo kasmāt. Dānādvā dyotnādvā. Dyu sthāno bhavati-ti vā

Why deva is so called? Because it has the nature to donate things to others, or it is located in the celestial sphere or it has its own light.

This way, all donors are called devas. All illuminating things are called devas and all celestial bodies are called devas. These devas are Devatā-s associated with Mantras of the Vedas. This proves that all sorts of donors: spiritual masters, teachers- the donors of knowledge, natural donors, celestial bodies, and all forms of energy are the subject matter of Mantras. All devatā-s are, in fact, are building blocks of this creation comprising of threefold nature: ādhyātmika (spiritual/metaphysical), ādhidaivika (astrophysical/ cosmological/ astronomical), and ādhibhautika/ laukika (belonging to the mundane world). As such, there is a parallelism in Devatā-s at ādhyātmika, ādhidaivika and ādhibhautika levels. For instance, Agni is one of the devatā. At ādhyātmika (spiritual/metaphysical) level, Agni denotes God, spiritual power. At ādhidaivika level, it represents energy, geothermal energy, stars, etc.

---

9. या तेनोच्यते सा देवता। *yā tenocyate sā devatā.*

At the ādhibhautika/laukika level it is fire on the earth, a person equipped with the power of knowledge like a teacher or a scholar, a person equipped with physical power like that of a king or commander. So, one single devatā denotes all its parallels at all the three levels. If one is able to decode a devatā, he is able to know the very meaning of a Mantra. Devatā, in fact, contains a key to the meaning of the Veda. Some scholars translate devatā as a god. But devatā is not a god in a literal sense. They all have a precise scientific meaning. They are fundamental particles and forces of nature in ādhidaivika sense, spiritual forces in ādhyātmika sense, and mundane life articles or things in ādhibhautika/laukika sense. Some scholars try to draw human history from the Vedas, but there is no human history in the Vedas.

Devatās are located at three regions, the observer space (Pṛthivī), the intermediate space (Antarikṣa), and the light space (Dyau). The devatā-s located in the observer space are represented by Agni (matter particles). The devatā-s located in the intermediate space are represented by Vāyu (field energy) and devatā-s located in the light space are represented by Āditya/Sūrya (massless energy/photons). Other devatas located in three spaces are different forms of Agni, Vāyu, and Āditya (Sūrya).

Yāska (*Nirukta*, 7.5), an ancient Vedic scholar points out this fact as:

तासां महाभाग्याद् एकैकस्य अपि बहूनि नामधेयानि भवन्ति। अपि वा कर्म पृथक्त्वात्।

tāsāṁ mahābhāgyādekai-kasya'pi bahūni nāmadheyāni bhavanti. api vā karma pṛthaktvāt.

That is due to different characters or functions, one single devatā is known by different names.

Śaunaka, the author of *Bṛhaddevatā* (1.70), bears out the same fact as:

एतासामेव महात्म्यान नामान्यत्वं विधीयते।

तत् तत् स्थान विभागेन तत्र तत्रेह दृश्यते।।

etāsāmeva mahātmyān nāmānyatvaṁ vidhiyate
tat-tat-shthāna vibhāgena tatra tatreha dṛśyate.

Due to different characteristics, they are named differently at different locations.

See also

तासामियं विभूतिर्हि नामानि यदनेकसः।

आहुस्तासां तु मन्त्रेषु कवयोऽन्योऽन्ययोनिताम्।।

tāsāmiyaṁ vibhūtirhi nāmāni yadanekaśaḥ.
āhustāsāṁ tu mantreṣu kavayo' nyo'nyayonitām.
Bṛhaddevatā (1.71)

Due to various functions, one devatā finds various names.

For example, in observer space, Agni is the main devatā and Jātavedas, Vaiśvānara, Draviṇodā, Tanunapāt Nārāsaṁsa, llā, Vṛṣabha, etc. etc. are subordinate to or various forms of Agni[10].

Similarly, in intermediate space, Indra and Vayu are

---

10 See अग्निः पृथिवी स्थानः *agniḥ prithivī sthānaḥ-* (*Nir.* 7.5)

अथैतान्यग्निभक्तिनि। अयं लोकः प्रातःस्वनम्। वसन्तः गायत्री त्रिवृत्स्तोम रथन्तरसाम। ये च देवगणाः स्माम्नाता प्रथमे स्थाने।

athaitānyagnibhaktīni. ayam lokaḥ prāthsavanam,
vasantaḥ, gāyatrī, trivṛtstoma, rathantaram sāma,
ye ca devagaṇāḥ samāmnātāḥ prathame sthāne. Nir. 7.8

See also *Bṛhaddevatā* 1.73-अग्निडिस्मन ,*agni'smin.*

Also

यद्यत्र पृथिवीस्थानं पार्थिवं चाग्निमाश्रितम्। तदसर्वमनुपूर्व्येण कथ्यमानं निबोधत्।

yadyatra prithivīsthānaṁ pārthivaṁ cāgnimāṣritam
tadasarvamanu pūrvyeṇa kathyamānaṁ nibodhat.
(Bṛd. 1.105. Cf. also 1.106-1.120).

the main devatās and Parjanya, Rudra, Bṛhaspati,

---

11 As to the principal deities, see *Nirutka* (7.5)

वायवेन्द्रो वान्तरिक्षस्थानः।

vāyavendrovāntarik-ṣasthānaḥ.

And *Bṛhaddevatā* (7.73) : अथेन्द्रस्तु मध्यतो वायुरेव च। *athendrastu madhyato vāyureva ca.*

As to co-deities see *Nir.* (7.10) :

अथेतानिन्द्र भक्तिनि अन्तरिक्षलोकः, माध्यन्दिनं स्वनम्, ग्रीष्मः, त्रिष्टुप, पंचदशस्तोमः, बृहत्साम, ये देवगणाः समाम्नाता मध्यमे स्थाने याश्च स्त्रियः।

athetānīndra bhaktīni antarikṣalokaḥ, mādhyandinaṁ savanam, grıṣmaḥ, trıṣṭup, pañcadaśastomaḥ, bṛhatsām, ye devagaṇāh samāmnātā madhyame sthāne yāśca striyaḥ.

Also *Bṛd.* from 1.121- यश्चेन्द्रो मध्यमस्थानोगणः सोऽयमतः परः।

yaścaindro madhyamasthānogaṇaḥ so' yamataḥ paraḥ to 2.6.

12. As to the principal deities, see *Nir.* (7.5) सूर्यो द्युस्थानः

sūryo dyusthānaḥ;

Also *Bṛhad.* (2.7): यः परस्तु सौर्यो द्युस्थानस्तं निबोधत्

yaḥ parastu sauryo dyusthānastaṁ nibodhat.

For co-deities, see Nir. (7.10) -

अथैतान्यादित्य भक्तिनि असौ लोकः, तृतीयस्वनम्, वर्षा जगति, सप्तदश स्तोमः, वैरूप्यं साम, ये चे देवगणाः समाम्नाता उत्तमे स्थाने यश्च स्त्रियः।

athaitānyāditya bhaktīni asau lokaḥ, tṛtīyasavanaṁ, vaıṣ ā, jagati, saptadaśa stomaḥ, vairupaṁ sāma, ye ca devagaṇāḥ samāmnātā uttame sthāne yāś' ca striyaḥ.

See also *Bṛhad.* 2.8 to 2.16.

Apāṁnapāt, Pururavā, Aditiḥ, Tvaṣṭā, Savitā, Vāta, Vācaspati, Soma, Marut, Aṅgirasa, Ribhu, Pitara are subordinate to or different forms of Indra and Vāyu[11].

In the light space, Sūrya is the main devatā and Aśvinau, Vṛṣākapāyī, Sūryā, Uṣā, Pūṣā, Vṛṣākapi, Yama, Vaiśvānara, Viṣṇu, Varuṇa, Saptarṣi, Āditya, Savitā, etc. are subordinate to or different forms of Sūrya[12].

These devatā-s have been numbered 33 koṭis. Here the word koṭi is confusing. It has two meanings: '10 million' and 'type'. 33 Koṭi means 33 types. But, mistakenly koṭi was taken for '10 million'. Of the main 33 types of devatās, there are 8 Vasus in the observer space, 11 Rudras in the intermediate space, and 12 Ādityas in the light space with two more Mitra and Varuṇa. In this classification, Mitra and Varuna have a separate position.

There are a total of 951 Devatās in the four Vedas. The entire detail of these devatā-s has been given by the present author in his work 'Vedic Concordance of the Mantras as per Ṛṣi and Devatā'. This concordance in two vols. provide complete detail of the 951 Vedic Devatās.

The Chhanda (Metre)

As pointed out earlier, the Veda is the science of cosmology dealing with creation involving all its three aspects viz. *adhibhautika* (physical or geophysical aspect), *adhidaivika* (astronomical or astrophysical aspect) and *adhyātmika* (metaphysical or spiritual aspect). *Bhagvadgītā* (2.45) amply announces this character of the Veda as:

त्रैगुंण्यविषया वेदा

traiguṇyaviṣayā vedā

That is, the Vedas deal with the creation evolving out of the three *Guṇas* (*sattva*, *rajas,* and *tamas*) of Prakṛti.

These scientific mysteries of creation were unfolded through a scientific mode of documentation variously classified as *ṛcās*, *yajuṣas* and *sāmans*. The documentation in the form of *ṛcās* was known as the *Ṛgveda*, documentation in the form of *yajuṣas* was called as the *Yajurveda* and similarly documentation in the form of *sāmans* was known as the *Sāmaveda*. The technique and methodology of documenting the science of universal creation were also based on laws of universal creation. It is often quoted in the Vedic tradition that the documentation of the science of creation in the form of *ṛcās* was based on *agni*, i.e. geothermal energy. Agni (geothermal energy is called as a dominant factor of *Bhūloka* planets like earth. According to *Nirukta* (7.5), *Agni* (geothermal energy) is related to earth[13]. The documentation of science of creation in the form of *yajuṣas* was based upon *Vāyu* (field energy existing into the intermediate space). According to *Nirukta* (7.5), the *Vāyu* (Air) as energy is located in the intermediate space[14]. The documentation of science of creation in the form of *sāmans* was based upon *Sūrya* (solar energy) existing in the celestial space. According to the *Nirukta* (7.5), *Sūrya* (solar energy) is located in the celestial or light space[15].

Not only the *Nirukta*, but the *Śatapatha Brāhmaṇa* (11.5.8.3) also sheds an ample good light on the composition of the *Ṛgveda*, the *Yajurveda,* and the *Sāmaveda*. Accordingly, above mentioned three the Vedas came into existence on account of three forms of energy, i.e. the *Ṛgveda* came into being on account of *Agni* (geothermal energy), the *Yajurveda* came into being on account of *Vāyu* (air energy) and on account of *Sūrya* (solar energy) came into being the *Sāmaveda*.[i] The author

---

13 अग्निपृथिवीस्थानः। *agniḥ pṛthivi sthānaḥ.*

14 वायवेन्द्रो वान्तरिक्षस्थानः / *vāyavendro vāntrikṣasthānaḥ*

15 तेभ्यस्तप्तेभ्यस्त्रयो वेदाऽजायन्त।
अग्नेर्ऋग्वेदो वायोर्यजुर्वेदः सूर्यात्सामवेदः।

tebhyastaptebhyastrayo vedā ajāyanta.
agner ṛgvedo vāyor yajurvedaḥ sūryātsāmavedaḥ.

of this *Brāhmaṇa*, describes energy by the word *tapta* as:

तेभ्यस्तप्तेभ्यस्त्रयो वेदाऽजायन्त। अग्नेर्ऋग्वेदो वायोर्यजुर्वेदः सूर्यात्सामवेदः।

tebhyastaptebhyastrayo vedā ajāyanta.
agner ṛgvedo vāyor yajurvedaḥ sūryātsāmavedaḥ.

Out of three energies originated three the Vedas. From *Agni* (geothermal or observer space energy originated the *Ṛgveda*, from the field the *Yajurveda*, from the solar energy or light the *Sāmaveda*.

Manusmṛti also speaks the same language while dealing with the origin of the Vedas. According to *Manusmṛti*, '*Agni* (geothermal energy), *Vāyu* (field energy) and *Sūrya* (solar energy) are the main instruments behind the *Yajña* (the process of creation). The *Ṛgveda*, the *Yajurveda,* and the *Sāmaveda* originated on account of these energies[16].

The *Gopatha Brāhmaṇa* also associates *Agni* (geothermal energy/observer space energy) to the *Bhūloka* (earth/observer space), *Vāyu* (field energy) to the *Antarikṣ a-loka* (intermediate space) and *Sūrya* (solar energy/light) to the *Dyuloka* (celestial sphere/light space). Thus the whole creation on the earth gets summed up between the earth, the sun, and intervened by the intermediate space and the whole cosmic creation gets summed up between light space and observer space intervened by the intermediate space. The other way round we can say that the earth and the sun are interdependent for the creation on the earth. Keeping in view of this fact, the Vedas use the word *dyāvā-pṛthivī* time and again as a *Devatā Dvandva* compound. In fact, the interaction of solar energy with the geothermal energy causes the origin of life on the earth.

---

[16] अग्निवायुरविभ्यस्तुत्रयं ब्रह्मसनातनम्।
दुदोहयज्ञसिध्यर्थं ऋग्यजुसामलक्षणम्।

agni vāyu ravibhyastu trayaṁ brahma sanātanam
dudoha yajña-siddyarthaṁ ṛgyajuḥsāmalakṣaṇam.

This interaction is possible due to the earth's revolution around the sun. Thus the *Yajña* (the process of creation) on the earth is going on due to the joint participation of the earth and the sun.

When the earth moves around the sun, Sun's position in relation to earth changes with the change of every solar month (represented by a *Saṅkrānti*). The sun describes seven great circles of latitude on the earth during 12 months of a year. These seven great circles of latitude described by the sun are known as the seven major chhandas. The seven great circles of latitude or chhandas described by the sun on the earth are as follows:

23.5^0 circle of latitude south of the equator known as Tropic of Capricorn or the Gāyatrī Chhanda is caused by the sun when it transits through Makara (Capricorn) sign on 22nd December. This solar month is known in the Vedas as Aruṇa month.

The second circle of latitude described by the sun is 20^0 south of the equator. This circle is known in the Vedas as the Uṣṇika chhanda. It is caused by the sun during its transit through Kumbha and Dhanu signs on 21st January and 22nd Nov. respectively. The solar months formed on this chhanda are known in the Vedas as Aruṇarāja and Sambhara months.

The third circle of latitude described by the sun is 12^0 south of the equator. This circle is known in the Vedas as the Anuṣṭup chhanda. It is caused by the sun during its transit through the Mīna and the Vṛścika signs on 20th Feb and 23rd Oct. respectively. The solar months formed on this chhanda are known in the Vedas as Puṇḍarika and Sarvauṣ āḍha months.

The fourth circle of latitude described by the sun is 0^0 equator. This circle is known in the Vedas as the Bṛhati chhanda. It is caused by the sun during its transit through the Meṣa and Tulā signs on 21st March and 23rd Sept. respectively. The solar months formed on this chhanda are known in the Vedas as Viśvajita and Irāvān months.

The fifth circle of latitude described by the sun is 12^0 north of the equator. This circle is known in the Vedas as the Paṅkti chhanda. It is caused by the sun during its transit through the Vṛṣabha and the Kanyā signs on 21st April and 23rd August respectively. The solar months formed on this chhanda are known in the Vedas as Abhijita and Rasavān.

The sixth circle of latitude described by the sun is 20^0 north of the equator. This circle is known in the Vedas as the Triṣṭup chhanda. It is caused by the sun during its transit through the Mithuna and the Siṁha signs on 22nd May and 23rd July respectively. The solar months formed on this chhanda are known in the Vedas as Ārdrā and Unnavān months.

The seventh circle of latitude described by the sun is 23.5^0 north of the equator. This circle is known in the Vedas as the Jagati chhanda. It is caused by the sun during its transit through the Karka sign on 22nd June. The solar month formed on this chhanda is known in the Vedas as Pinvamāna month.

The process of describing seven chhandas is known in the Vedas as Vedī parigraha (Enclosing of the earth). In fact, this enclosure of the sun on the earth is known as chhanda. Etymologically also chhanda means enclosure: *chandāṁsi chādanāt.*

The *Yajurveda* (1.26) describes the sun's power of gravitation. The sun is gravitating the earth and encloses the earth with hundreds and thousands of rays.

देव सवितः परमस्यां पृथिव्यां शतेन पाशैः ।। □

In the next *Mantra* (*Yajurveda*, 1.27), three different enclosures of the sun on the south, west, and north of earth have been respectively described as Gāyatrī, Triṣṭubha, and Jagati chhanda.

गायत्रेण त्वा छन्दसा परिगृह्णमि

त्रैष्टुभेन त्वा छन्दसा परिगृह्णामि

जागतेन त्वा छन्दसा परिगृह्णामि

The *Śatapatha Brāhmaṇa* (1.2.5.1-13) gives a detailed commentary on this Mantra of the *Yajurveda* and illustrates a ritual of theVedī Parigraha (Enclosing of the Altar/earth). The ritual in the *Śatapatha Brāhmaṇa* reads as under:

> Having described the ritual of *stamba-yaju-haraṇa* (symbolising the dissipation the forces of darkness that are anti-creation forces, the ritual of 'Altar enclosing' representing various circles of latitude described by the sun along the earth are depicted here through a method of historical narration of the natural phenomenon.

The forces of light (instrumental in creation) and the forces of the darkness (anti-creation forces) both having originated from Prajāpati (a natural phenomenon of the rotation of the earth on its axis and its revolution around the sun), contended for superiority. In this contention for superiority, the forces of light (pro-creation forces) seemed to have been defeated by the forces of darkness. Since then the forces of darkness thought that this world belonged to them.

The forces of darkness, in view of their dominance, said, 'Let us share the earth with us, and having done so let us subsist upon it.' They set about sharing it with ox-hide from west to east (In the Indian context, after the rise of the sun in the east, there will be light east through west and the darkness will prevail from west to east. So it has been said that the forces of darkness set about sharing the earth from west to east).

The forces of the light (pro-creation forces) heard this and thought, 'The forces of darkness are actually dominating this earth. Let us go to the place where the forces of darkness are sharing the earth. What would become of us if we were deprived of our share? With the

Viṣṇu (the sun) as their head, they went there.'

They then said to the anti-creation forces of darkness, 'We may also be included in sharing the earth. Let there also be our share in it. The anti-creation forces of darkness could not tolerate it and told, 'As much place as this Viṣṇu (the sun) occupies through its circles of latitude (chhandas) on the earth, let only that much be yours.' Meaning to say, from 23.5^0 north to 23.5^0 south of the earth, the Viṣṇu (the sun) is visible. Rest of the parts remains in darkness.

Viṣṇu's (sun's) area on the earth (from 23.5^0 North to 23.5^0 South of equator) is very short. The forces of light, however, had no objection and accepted this proposal. 'Give us as much as is required for the Yajña (creation on earth), that will be sufficient for us.' said the forces of light. Thus from 23.5^0 North to 23.5^0 South of the equator became the part of the forces of light and rest became the part of forces of darkness.

The forces of light having laid down Viṣṇu, the sun on the eastward enclosed earth by various chhandas; 23½° south of the equator was enclosed with the Gāyatrī chhanda with the Yajurvedic Mantra, 'I enclose you by the Gāyatrī chhanda' (VS.1.27). Henceforth the tropic of the Capricorn is denoted by the Gāyatrī metre. (Note: the Gāyatrī metre has 24 syllables to denote 23½°). The western side with the Triṣṭup chhanda with the recitation of the Mantra, 'I enclose you with the help of Triṣṭup chhanda' (*VS.*1.27). Triṣṭubh being the next to Jagatī from west to east. The northern side with the Jagatī chhanda. 'I enclose you with the help of the Jagati chhanda' (*VS.*1.27). The tropic of cancer is denoted by the Jagatī metre. The Jagatī metre has 48 syllables, the double of 24 to represent 23½° N+23½° S.

Having enclosed the earth on all the sides with various chhandas (metre-ranges) and having ignited the fire of creation (sun) known as the Āhavanīya fire on the east side, the forces of light went on performing their work of creation with this fire and they occupied the whole of the earth along the tropics. Because they occupied the whole earth for the process of creation, this earth came to be known as Vedī (occupied one) or the altar as we may call it in terms of the English language. That is the reason why it is often said that the earth has the same parameters as those of the Vedī, for the sake of creation the entire earth was occupied by the pro-creation forces. And so one can wrest the entire earth from his rivals and can dispossess them of their share who realises this fact.

The Viṣṇu (sun) was bounded on all directions by the metres, with his head in the east direction. Thus unable to escape anywhere beyond tropical encompassment, i.e. beyond 23½° north and south of the equator (tropical zone), the Sun moved down to the roots of the vegetation.

The same narration is prolonged: The forces of light said, 'What has become of Viṣṇu? What has become of the Yajña, the natural process of creation?' They said, 'Enclosed on all sides by metres, with its head towards the east on the equator, there is no way of escaping; search for the Viṣṇu went on here itself.' They searched for it by slightly digging the earth. They discovered it at a depth of three fingers, i.e they found that the Viṣṇu has moved down the earth three circles of latitude 12^0, 20° and 23.5^0 north and south of the equator. Therefore the Vedī (altar) should be made three fingers deep. In view of the same fact, a scholar named Pāñci made the earth three fingers deep.

But this should not be done. Since the Viṣṇu (Sun) moved the earth to the extent of the roots of the vegetations, so let him (the Adhvaryu) ask the Āgnidhra to cut out the roots of the vegetation. And because they found Viṣṇu in a tropical region, so they called the tropics as an altar.

Having found Viṣṇu at the first cardinal point, i.e. 23½° north and south of the equator, they enclosed him with a second enclosure, i.e at 20° north and south of the equator. On the north with the text (*VS.*1.27), 'You are of good soil and auspicious.' On the 20° south when the forces of light discovered Viṣṇu, they made the earth of good soil and auspicious. (The part of the earth around 20° south of the equator is fertile and auspicious). On the west, it was enclosed with the text (*VS.*1.27), 'The pleasant and comfortable to sit upon you are.' Having thus located Viṣṇu on the west side of the earth, they made that part of the earth pleasant and comfortable to sit upon. On the 20° north the Viṣṇu was enclosed with the text (*VS.*1.27), 'Abounding in food and water are you.' Having discovered Viṣṇu on 20° north, they made part of the earth prosperous in food and water. (We can see the rivers originating from the north).

The Viṣṇu thus draws three enclosures before the equator, i.e. at the points of 23½°, 20°, 12° south and three after the equator, i.e. 23½°,20°, 12° north of the equator. These all enclosures together make six. So are made the six seasons of the year. A year is the time process (Yajña) of creation (Prajāpati). As large is the yearly process of creation, so wide as its (tropical movement of the sun) extent is between the tropics. So, widely, he (the Adhvaryu) thereby encloses this fire altar.

With six vyāhṛtis (the parts of the Mantras) he draws the first six enclosures representing the northward six tropical movements of the sun during the six months of Uttarāyaṇa, i.e.

a). 23½° S to 20° S

b). 20° S to 12° S

c). 12° S to 0°

d). 0° to12° N

e). 12° N to 20° N

f). 20° N to 23½° N and with the six vyāhṛtis, he draws the second six enclosures representing the reverse course, i.e. southward six movements of the sun during the six months of Dakṣīṇāyana period. This makes these together twelve, and thus twelve are made the solar months of the year. The year is the process of the creation. As large is the yearly process of creation, so wide is the tropical movements of the Sun between the tropics. So widely, he (the Adhvaryu) thereby encloses this fire altar.

Thus from the aforementioned description of the ritual of Altar enclosure, it is crystal clear that the sun encloses earth at seven tropical lines which are known by the name of seven famous chhandas or circles of latitude.

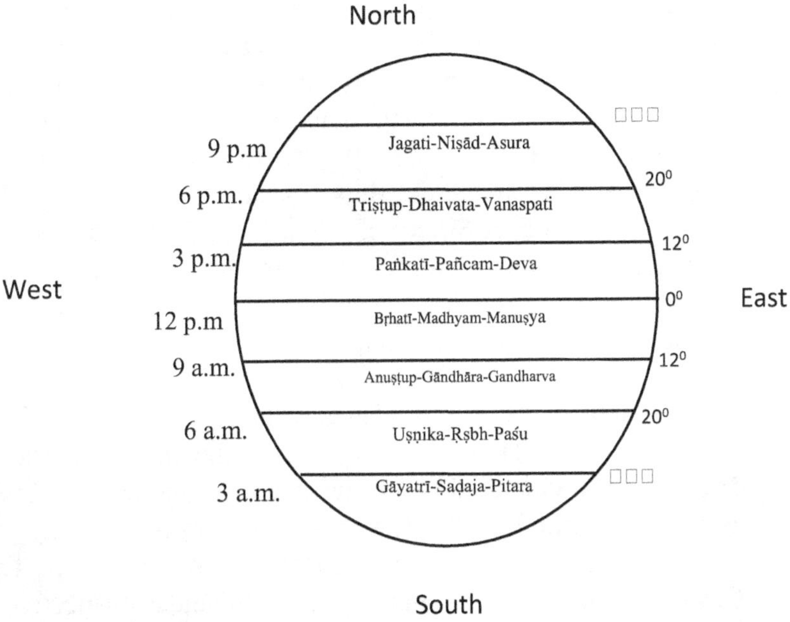

The above-given diagram makes the above descriptions explicitly clear.

These tropical movements of the sun are caused by earth's 23.5^0 North-west inclination on its axis.

Here it may also be informed that with the Sun's enclosure of the Gāyatrī chhanda, Uttarāyaṇa, i.e. North or winter solstice commences. The Uttarāyaṇa or winter solstice pointed out the beginning of the year. In fact, during the Vedic age, it was also the Devayāna period, due to the Indian continent's location being in the Kumeru, i.e. Southern hemisphere of the earth. So the Gāyatrī chhanda has a great significance, being the southernmost point of the sun's enclosure on the earth. It was the sun's appearance on the earth that caused the emergence of biological life on this planet. At the beginning of the Kalpa, the Gāyatrī cover used to take place in the Makara (Capricorn) sign. These days it takes place in the Dhanu (Sagittarius) sign on Dec. 22.

Keeping in view of the same phenomenon of nature, the documentation of the *Ṛgveda* took place. The Mantras of the *Ṛgveda* were also composed in seven metres representing the seven parigrahas or enclosures of the sun on the planet earth. First is the Gāyatrī metre which consists of 24 syllables thus exactly representing the number of 23.5^0. Since .5 (half) number cannot be represented by a syllable, so .5 (half) was counted for one and the no. 24 has been assigned to the Gāyatrī chhanda. If we take up the last parigraha, i.e. Jagatī chhanda, we find it just opposite to the Gāyatrī, i.e. $23.5\ ^0$ N of the equator. Thus the total distance of the Jagatī from the Gāyatrī is $23.5\ ^0$ S to $23.5\ ^0$ N, i.e. 24 + 24 = 48. Now one may not find it difficult to understand why the Jagatī chhanda has been assigned the number of 48. In other words, this is only the reason that the Jagatī chhanda consists of 48 syllables. The Gāyatrī through Jagatī, there lie five chhandas respectively as the Uṣṇika, the Anuṣṭup, the Bṛhatī, the Paṅktī and the Triṣṭup. The numbers between 24 and 48 can be divided proportionally into 7 segments each one with an increment of 4 numbers, e.g. 24, 28, 32, 36, 40, 44, 48. As such no. 24 and 48 having been already assigned to the first (the Gāyatrī) and last (the Jagatī) chhandas, the intervening nos. 28, 32, 36, 40, 44 can be assigned respectively to the intervening five chhandas, i.e. no. 28 to the Uṣṇika, no. 32 to the Anuṣṭup, no. 36 to the Bṛhatī, no. 40 to the Paṅktī and no. 44 to the Triṣṭup. This is the reason why the Vedic seers assigned the above-mentioned sequence of nos. to the various chhandas.

Thus from the foregoing discussion, it is clear that the Vedic metres are not just like ordinary literary metres applied to the compositions of various literary genres. The phenomena of chhanda applied to the Vedic lore has its astronomical base. That is why metres, in the Vedas, have been called as Daivī prajā, or the divine compositions. chandaṁsi vai daivyḥ prajāḥ, i.e. metres in the Vedas represent the divine or astronomical phenomena. As it has already been pointed out above that the chhandas in the Veda are related with the tropical movements of the sun on the earth. So, the first Gāyatrī chhanda represents the first prahara of the day starting at 3 a.m. This is the rising period of the sun. That is why the Vedic seer eulogises the sun through the Gāyatrī Mantra composed in Gāyatrī chhanda. The famous Gāyatrī Mantra reads as follows:

तत्सवितुर्वरेण्यं भर्गो देवस्य धीमहि। धियो यो नः प्रचोदयात्।।

tat savitur vareṇyam bhargo devasya dhīmahi.
dhīyo yo naḥ pracodayāt.

'That we meditate upon the effulgence of the rising sun, the generator of the world, which is worthy to be adopted. This rising sun makes all the living beings swing into various actions.'

Vedic Chhandas (Metres)

The above-cited 7 cosmic chhandas were used as major chhandas in the documentation of Vedic Mantras. The cosmic latitudinal degrees of the above chhandas was taken as syllable count for the Vedic Mantras. For instance,

Gāyatrī chhanda has 24 syllables

Uṣṇika chhanda has 28 syllables

Anustup chhanda has 32 syllables

Bṛhatī chhanda has 36 syllables

Paṅkti chhanda has 40 syllables

Triṣṭup chhanda has 44 syllables

Jagatī chhanda has 48 syllables

On the same pattern giving an increment of 4 syllables each, seven more chhandas were formed by the Vedic Ṛṣis. They are as follows:

Atijagati 52 syllables

Śakvarī 56 syllables

Atiśakvarī 60 syllables

Aṣṭi 64 syllables

Atyaṣṭi 68 syllables

Dhṛti 72 syllables

Atidhṛti 76 syllables

Here it may be pointed out that the syllable count of the Mantras was not always exactly the same as cited above. We sometimes come across Mantras having one or two syllables less or more than the specified count of the chhandas. We may find Gāyatrī chhanda not necessarily with 24 syllables, it may have 23, 22, 25 or 26 syllables also. Such cases have been given different names. According to Kātyāyana, if a Mantra has one syllable less or more than the specified count of a chhanda, the chhanda will be called Nichṛd and Bhūrik respectively. Thus Gāyatrī chhanda with 23 syllables will be known as Nichṛd Gāyatrī and with 25 syllables will be known as Bhūrik Gāyatrī.

Similarly, if a Mantra has two syllables less or more than the specified count of a chhanda, the chhanda will be called Virāṭ and Svarāṭ respectively. Thus Gāyatrī with 22 syllables will be called Virāṭ Gāyatrī and with 26 syllables as Svarāṭ Gāyatrī.

In addition to the above, we find many other varieties of the chhandas like Kakup, Pada Paṅkti, Vardhmāna, Pratiṣṭha etc. in the Veda Mantras, but they are insignificant.

Vedic Svaras (Grammatical)

There are two types of svaras used in the Vedas. They are 1. Grammatical, 2. musical. Today we shall deal with only grammatical svaras.

Grammatical Svaras

There are three types of grammatical svaras.

1. उदात्त Udaatta: Acute accent (or high accent
2. अनुदात्त Unudaatta: Grave accent or low accent
3. स्वरित Svarita: Circumflexed accent or middle accent

Generally, the syllables that have udātta or acute accent or high accent are called accented, if they have unudātta accent or low accent, they are called unaccented. In a Vedic word, only one syllable may be accented. Because a word is formed of root+suffix, so there may broadly be two options of accentuation in a word:

1. A word may have an acute accent, either on its root or on the suffix.

2. It may also remain unaccented at all, e.g verbal forms generally remain unaccented and nominal forms in vocative case (address) remain unaccented.

Now one may ask a question as to how to identify accented syllables, unaccented syllables, and syllables having middle/svarita accent in Vedic words. The answer is in different Vedas different accentuation patterns are followed. For example, in the Rigveda, an accented syllable or a syllable with udātta accent remains unmarked. An unaccented syllable is underlined and a syllable with svarita accent has a vertical line over it.

Example is अग्निमी□ळे पुरोहि□तम्

In Sāmaveda, accents are marked with a numeral or with numeral and letter above the syllable. Udātta, Anudātta, and Svarita are marked with numerals 1, 2, and 3 respectively over the syllable. In addition to numerals 1,2,3 we see letters र (ra), क (ka) and उ (u) placed over the syllables along with numerals. We illustrate one:

If two udāttas occur in sequence, then the first udātta is

represented by numeral 1 and second is not represented by any numeral, but the svarita that follows the second udātta is indicated by 2र. Syllables that have no numeral or letters above them are called prachaya.

The *Yajurveda* and the *Atharvaveda* follow the Rigvedic pattern of accentuation.

Note: In roman script, the accent is represented by a slanting line over the syllable, e.g. *á*

Pronunciation of different accents

These svaras have three different patterns of pronunciation.

1. Udātta accent: According to Pāṇini, a great Sanskrit grammarian, udātta accent is pronounced from higher parts of the place of articulation of its syllable.
2. Anudātta accent is pronounced from the lower parts of the place of articulation of its syllable.
3. Svarita accent is pronounced from the middle parts of the place of articulation of its syllable.

Vedas may be recited with an accent. Such a recitation of Vedic mantras is known as **Sasvara Pāṭha**. Vedas may also be recited without svara. This recitation is known as **Ekaśruti Savara Pāṭha** which is possible after a lot of practice. Only traditional Vedic Pandits can recite mantras with svara, as it requires a lot of training and practice. It can be done under the supervision of a trained Guru.

Accent as a Morphological and Semantic Determinant

Be aware that an accent plays a significant role in determining the nature of morphological features like noun, pronoun, verb, indeclinable, etc. in case of ambiguity created by their analogous forms and other compound forms. This may also help analyzing a true meaning of the concerned morphological feature and compound words. To illustrate it, a few examples may be cited:

1. There are two analogous forms: *kaḥ* (a pronominal form i.e. masculine singular nominative form of pronoun *kim*) and *kaḥ* (a verbal form from root √kṛ . In this case, the only accent helps the determination of the true nature of *kaḥ* . *kaḥ* as a verbal form remains unaccented, otherwise if accented, i.e. *káḥ*, it will be a pronominal form.

2. There is an interesting mantra from the *Yajurveda* (32.3) which reads as under:

न तस्य□ प्रति‍मा अ□स्ति।

nátasya pratimaa asti

In this mantra, *nátásya* has been a bone of contention among scholars. This may be read as a single word *nátásya* or the composition of two words *ná+tásya.* If it is read as a single word, its meaning would be -The God Who is submissive to His devotees, has His picture. If it is regarded as a composition of two words *ná+tásya,* its meaning would be -There is no picture of God. These two are very much debated and discussed meanings, the solution of which depends upon the determination of the nature of the word *nátásya.* Here the accent comes for our help. According to the rule of accentuation, a word can carry only one acute accent. In *nátásya,* as is obvious, *ná* and *tá* both are accented which shows that both are parts of two different words: *ná* and *tásya* put in a single whole *nátásya.*

Thus, the knowledge of svara is very important and one of the keys to understand the intended meaning of Vedas

Vedic Svara (Musical)

In addition to the grammatical svaras, which are significant in determining the nature of words and their meanings, Vedic chhandas are attuned to some Musical notes for the purpose of recitation. Different chhandas are recited with different musical notes. These musical notes are natural and not artificially composed as is the case with modern-day musical notes. At different timings, the nature emits different vibrations. These vibrations are svaras of nature. Different timings represented by different svaras are as under:

1. The time from 3 am to 6 am is represented by "aÇaja svara
2. The time from 6 am to 9 am is represented by ÿ–bha svara
3. The time from 9 am to 12 Noon is represented by GÈndhÈra svara
4. The time from 12 Noon to 3 pm is represented by Madhyam svara
5. The time from 3 pm to 6 pm is represented by Pa¤cam svara
6. The time from 6 pm to 9 pm is represented by Dhaivata svara
7. The time from 9 pm to 12 O clock night is represented by Ni–Èd svara

From 9 pm to 3 am the nature also sleeps for six hours. That is why the sleeping timings for average human beings have been fixed for 6 hours. The Vedas say that every human being should go to sleep at 9 pm and rise in Brahma Muhurta i.e. 3 am. At that time the nature emits a nectar-like breeze and a person who develops the habit of going to bed between 9 pm to 3 am in consonance with nature will live a hale and hearty life.

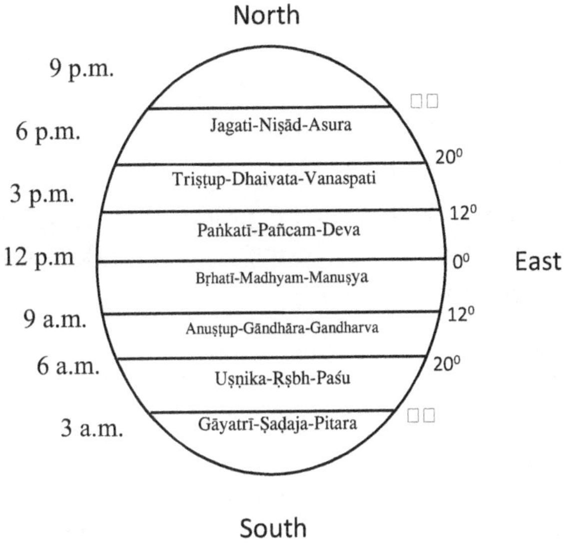

Meters and Their Musical Notes

The Gāyatrī chhanda is recited in Ṣaḍaja svara. Gāyatrī chhanda being the sixth one when counted from the Jagatī side, its svara has been called as Ṣaḍaja. This chhanda belongs to the region of Pitaras, i.e. 23.5^0 S of equator being known as pitṛloka. Moreover, in Gāyatrī mantra, the Sun is eulogized as Savitā, i.e. the creator of the world, similarly the pitaras (ancestors of human beings) were the first originator of humanity and the Indian continent tenanting the Southern hemisphere was the first abode of human beings first ever born on the Earth. These first human beings were the parents of the rest of human beings. That is why, the Gāyatrī chhanda has been associated with the pitṛ-loka, i.e. the ancestral abode or the place of first-ever born parents or pitaras. Uṣṇika chhanda, being the second one in sequence, represents the second prahara (watch) starting at 6 am. This period is hotter as compared to the period of 3 am. Similarly 20^0 South of the equator i.e. Tropic of Aquarius being the hotter region as compared to the 23.5^0 South of the equator, i.e. Tropic of Capricorn. That is why the metre representing the period of 6 pm and the region of 20^0 South of the equator was christened as Uṣṇika chhanda. Moreover, 20^0 South of the equator had thick forest growth on the Earth. The forest region of the South was known as paśu whereas the forest region of the Northern hemisphere was called as the Vanaspati loka. Due to the dense forest belt, the region was famous as paśu loka.

The Uṣṇika chhanda is pronounced in ṛṣabha svara. Since this chhanda belongs to the animal world, its svara (musical note) is called as ṛṣabha.

The Anuṣṭup chanda, being the third one in sequence, represents the third prahara (watch) of the day starting at 9 p.m. The mid-day time and middle part of the Earth represented by Bṛhatī chhanda is known as stoma. Since this chhanda follows the stoma chhanda, it is named as Anuṣṭup (meaning anu-stoma). This chhanda belongs to the region of Gandharvas. Present-day, this region falls in Afganistan and is known as Kandhar. During the Vedic period, when the Indian continent was tenanting the Southern hemisphere, Gāndhāra used to be located at 12^0 South of equator. So, the region of 12^0 South of equator was also known as Gāndhāra region. And the musical note for pronouncing Anuṣṭup chhanda was also christened as Gāndhāra.

Bṛhatī chhanda represents the middle part of the Earth, i.e. equatorial region. It also represents the fourth prahara (watch) of the day starting at mid-day, i.e. 12 p.m. So, the musical note assigned to this metre was named as Madhyama svara. Since the equatorial region of the Earth remained densely populated by human-beings, this region was known as Manuṣya loka.

Counting Gāyatrī as the first chhanda, the fifth chhanda comes to be Paṅkatī. This is why its name is Paṅktī, the fifth one. The musical note assigned to it is also christened as Pañcam, the fifth one. It belongs to the region opposite to Gandharva loka, i.e. 12^0 North of equator which was geographically known as Devaloka.

From Bṛhatī, i.e. first stoma onward third one is called as Triṣṭup, i.e. third stoma. Its region is opposite to that of Uṣ ṇika, i.e. 20^0 North of equator which, being the forest belt of the Earth, is known as the Vanaspati loka. Its svara is Dhaivata. It represents the time period of the sixth prahara (watch), i.e. 6 p.m.

The last one is the Jagatī chhanda which represents the Asura region, i.e. $23.5\ ^0$ North of equator. Likewise, it also represents the 7th prahara, i.e. the period of 9 p.m. Its svara is known as Niṣāda.

All these musical notes are pronounced in various tones depending upon the time period they denote or represent. For instance, Niṣāda and Gāndhāra represent respectively the time period of 9 p.m. and 9 a.m. The number of 9 being the highest one in the series, and the physical energy being at its peak level both at 9 p.m. and 9 a.m., both the svaras are pronounced with high (udātta) tone. On the other hand, Ṛṣ abha and Dhaivata being the representative of 6 a.m. and 6 p.m. respectively or say next one to follow Niṣāda and Gāndhāra in point of numbers, they are pronounced in a low tone or the tone following udātta (i.e. anudātta) tone. The rest of the three, i.e. Ṣaḍaja, Madhyama and Pañcama being the representative of 3 am, mid-day and 3 pm respectively are pronounced with the middle tone or mixed tone of the prior two and technically known as svarita tone.

Authorship of the Vedas

There has long been a debate as to whether Vedas were created by God or man. It has always been answered: *vedāḥ apauruṣeyāḥ*, i.e. Vedas are not expressed by *Puruṣa* (some human being), but here the term *Puruṣa* has been taken up for both the meanings, i.e. for man as well as for God by the various contenders in order to support their contentions. Here it may be pointed out that the term Puruṣ a here does not mean God but man. So the term '*vedāḥ apauruṣeyāḥ*' would only mean 'Vedas are not created by human beings'.

The other way round also, the Veda being knowledge, or *dharma* would reside permanently in its *dharmī*, the object, the consciousness, or say consciousness being qualified by knowledge can be considered as its creator. Thus knowledge is the inherent quality of God.

Moreover, it can again be proved on the evidences gathered from the Vedic literature. For example, the *Śatapatha Brāhmaṇa* (14.5.4.10) has made a clear cut statement that the Vedas are the expressions of creation. Accordingly :

> 'The couplets that are known as *Ṛgveda*, *Yajuveda*, *Sāmveda* and *Atharvaveda* are the exhalations of the created world.'[17]

At another place in the same work, it has been clearly picturized leaving no space for further doubt and suspense regarding the Godly origin of Vedas. According to the *Śatapatha Brāhmaṇa* (11.5.4.17) :

> 'There are two types of creations. One is the human creation produced through the sexual behaviour. Another is the divine or cosmic creation. *Chandas*

[17] *evaṁ vā are'sya mahato bhūtasya niḥśvasitam-etad-va ṛegvedo yajurveda sāmaveda'tharvāṅgirasaḥ.*

deal with the cosmic creation. They are produced by *ṛṣis* through their mouth. Instead of sexual behaviour, they are produced verbally from the mouth by *devas* or scholars to define the universal creation of God'.[18]

Thus from the forgoing discussion, it can unhesitatingly be inferred that the couplets or Chandas revealed to various Vedic seers were the literary items originated first ever in the literary history of humankind. These chandas that dealt with the cosmic creation of God were pronounced by the ṛṣ is through their mouth.

Here Gitā's views on Vedas may also be quoted. Gītā says: *triguṇavıṣayo vedaḥ,* i.e. the Vedas deal with the *triguṇātmaka prakṛti.* The material creation evolved out of the disharmony of three guṇas : *sattva*, *rajas* and *tamas.*

The above view and Gītā's view on Vedas clearly points out that Vedas are the knowledge of creation. And the creation is the handy work of the almighty God. As such the knowledge of the Vedas can be called as the knowledge of the God and not the knowledge of a human being. For example, when an engineer invents an engine, the knowledge of the engine is the knowledge of the engineer. A potter makes a pot. Knowledge of the pot is the knowledge of the potter. Similarly, knowledge of the creation enshrined in the Vedas is the knowledge of the God.

---

[18] *dvayāḥ vā imāḥ prajā daivyaścaiva mānuṣyaśca. tā vā imā mānusyaḥ prajāḥ mithunād prajāyante. chandāṁsi vai daivyaḥ prājās-tāni mukhato janayate tata etaṁ janayate.*

Age of the Vedas

The age of the Vedas is a hotly debated issue. Scholars from time to time have been engaged in determining the antiquity of this oldest literature of the world. In fact, in determining the date of the Vedas, scholars have been led by their various pre-conceived notions and true or false beliefs. Whereas occidental scholars have their own sets of notions and beliefs, oriental scholars have theirs own. Obsessed with their different types of beliefs and notions the age-old Vedic tradition has totally been ignored or given a goodbye. It was always argued by various scholars at home and abroad that the Vedic traditional belief is clearly very speculative and based on fictitious astronomical calculations. The fact is that none of the viewpoints, occidental or oriental considered as non-speculative has any scientific basis, rather they are also based on speculations more dangerous and misleading than what is called traditional one.

The so-called scientific viewpoint of occidental scholars was based upon their assumption of the origin of the universe and thereby the origin of humans on the earth. In the 16th century, an Archbishop named Usher (1581-1656) thoughtlessly declared that creation took place on 22 October, 4004 years before the birth of Christ.

Archbishop Usher

Since the clergymen were the religious teachers and guides of the western scholars, in the light of such statements westerners started making surmises regarding the possible antiquity of the world's ancient most literature. When the date of creation was fixed as 4004 years before Christ, the date of the origin of the first book in the library of the world could also not be stretched beyond the date of creation. Based upon this framework of time, western scholars started their pursuit to determine the date of the origin of the Vedas.

It was presumed by most of the European scholars that the ancient most Ṛgvedic hymns must have been composed of about c1500 B.C. to c1000 B.C. Macdonell (1854-1930) thinks that the first collection which was again edited about c600 B.C. after making phonetic changes or *Sandhis* sanctioned by Classical Sanskrit (p.50) comes from a period which can hardly be less remote than c1000 B.C. (p.48). Max Müller (1823-1900) first assigned these dates from a consideration of the linguistic changes discernible in the language of the oldest hymns and the language of Pāṇini. He thought that there were thus several linguistic layers, so to speak, discernible through the Vedic literature and each layer might be assigned a period of about 200 years. Fixing the date of Pāṇini at 300 B.C., he assigned about c1500 B.C. as the probable date of the oldest Ṛgvedic hymns. As some of the hymns exactly correspond with some gāthās of the Avesta, it is also thought that the Iranians and Indians separated about this period and the bulk of the Ṛgvedic hymns was composed thereafter in Punjab. Thus, according to the most western scholars, the age of the *Ṛgveda* ranges between c1500 to c1000 B.C. But now the Usher's date of creation of the earth has completely collapsed in wake of modern scientific discoveries. According to new estimates, the earth is more than 400 crore years old and so the earlier speculations assigning the Vedas a date between c1500 to c1000 B.C. in the light of the old view of the creation became totally false and ungrounded. Under the circumstances when the basic assumptions have been disapproved by the scientific discoveries, there is no room left for the consideration of the speculations based on such shattered assumptions.

The Second view is held by many Indian scholars, led by Bal Gangadhara Tilak. They assign a far different antiquity to the Vedas based upon astronomical events referred to here and there in the Vedic and allied literature. But the main problem with these scholars is that they are very selective while dilating upon the Vedas or ancient Sanskrit literature. They are ready to accept the part statement of the Vedas as suitable to their pre-conceived notions and projections about the so-called dating of the ancient Sanskrit literature. They are not ready to accept the tradition as a whole. According to these scholars Rama's birth during the period when vernal equinox was taking place in the Punarvasu nakṣatra is acceptable, but to them, the beginning of the Tretā period mentioned in the same tradition is not acceptable, rather they venture to call such statements as mere suppositions. They don't seem to have the patience to wait and watch the further developments in the field of science. They forget that if the mention of the Tretā or the Dvāpara or the Satyayuga is speculative, the mention of the Punarvasu or Aśvini or Kṛttikā may also be speculative. They have, in fact, no basis or evidence to accept one part as confirmed and another part as fictitious. They are ready to accept the historical events of the *Rāmāyaṇa* or the *Mahābhārata* (*Mbh.*) taking place in this country, but they are reluctant to accept the antiquity of *Mbh.* as handed down to us in a long uninterrupted tradition of 5119 years.

Thus they are doubtful about themselves and also misleading other readers and scholars. If they want to accept the part of the tradition, why they don't accept the whole tradition. If something is beyond the ambit of their comprehension, they should make it a point of further research and study, instead of discarding the whole phenomena as fictitious. Modern researches into astronomy and astrophysics have proved the phenomenon of precession to be true and there is no denying the fact that equinoctial points and solstitial points continue to recede completing the whole circle in 25920 years.

Under the circumstances when the same phenomenon of equinoctial or solstitial precession repeat itself in 25920 years, there is no problem in accepting the *Yuga* and the *Manvantara* theory mentioned in the Vedic and Puranic literature, so as to ascertain the actual circle of equinoctial or solstitial points.

The third concept is the traditional Indian view, according to which the Vedas were composed at the time of the creation. Since the Vedas are the knowledge of creation, this knowledge came into existence in the universe at the very moment of its creation. This may be illustrated by an example of a machine. When an engineer makes a machine, the knowledge of machine comes into existence in the cosmos at the very moment of its creation. So, the traditional view maintained that the Vedas, the knowledge of creation were authored by God himself at the beginning of creation. The period of creation is calculated to be 197 crores (1.9 billion) years which is handed down to us in the tradition of the *Saṁkalpa Pāṭhas.* The socio-linguistic survey of Vedic and Puranic literature done by the author of present lines all but prove the authenticity of the antiquity of the Indian era handled in the long and uninterrupted tradition of *Saṁkalpa Pāṭha.*

Some facts on this issue are rendered hereunder:

Antiquity of the Vedic Era - A Test of Authenticity

The comparative study of the various eras of the world leads one to conclude that it is only the ancient Indian era or the *Bhāratīya Kālagaṇanā* which is the longest in the world. All other eras of the world, which are quite the latest as compared to the Vedic era are either based on great personalities, dynasties, or some important events. In fact, the great seers of India did not consider individuals, dynasties, or events important, but according to them a time or *Kāla* was above all. Everything in this world is encapsulated in time and time is independent of all. So, according to them, personalities or events were to be studied from the point of time and it was not the time that was to be studied from the point of personalities, dynasties, or events.

The Indian era which is known as the Kalpa era or Srṣṭi era has the remotest antiquity of 197 crore years. This era has unanimously been accepted in the *Vedaṅgas,* the *Purāṇas,* and the *Manusmṛti,* etc. Presently this era has come down to us as Kali era 5118. In fact, only this era was prevalent in India through ages, except a few others which came into vogue after 3000 years of the commencement of present Kaliyuga. These later evolved eras are also based, like the most of the others in the world, on some personalities, dynasties, or events. Mention may be made of the Vikram era of 57 B.C., originally called the Mālava era, and the next noted era is that of the Śakas commencing with 78 A.D. The Traikuṭaka (249 A.D.) and the Gupta (319 A.D.) eras followed in 3rd and 4th centuries A.D. It seems probable that the Indians got the idea of naming an era after some personality or dynasty or event from the foreigners who came in their contact. Their original era which was safeguarded in the tradition of the Saṁkalpa pāṭhas since 197 crore years till date is based purely on astronomical calculations. It begins with the beginning of the Kalpa and so-called as the Kalpa era. In fact, this era has been handed down to us with the utmost accuracy by a tradition of the Vedic people.

According to some scholars, this era is hypothetical and fictitious based on astronomical calculations of ancient Indian astrologers. Had there been any such era in currency, there would have been chronological data in the

Ṛgvedic hymns. But these arguments are baseless. In fact, there were two different but parallel traditions. One was the Vedic and the other was the Paurāṇika tradition. Whereas Vedic tradition preserved the Vedas (knowledge of creation), the Paurāṇika tradition preserved the Kālagaṇanā (the time period of creation), genealogies, and the history of creation and decreation.

The Vedas are the books of knowledge and science and so their purpose was not to record the chronology like the present-day books on sciences and technology. Moreover, we come across repeated mention of the Manvantara and the yugas in the Purāṇas and other works, which obviously point out the various phases of chronology. The Indian era tells about the chronology of millions of years. The number of years is so extensive that it is not feasible to keep the chronological record of all the past events. We had an age-old tradition of the *Itihāsa* and *Purāṇa.* The tradition of the *Purāṇas* is still extant whereas the tradition of the *Itihāsa* has lost its existence due to some catastrophic reasons or other. No documentary proof of the same is now available for demonstration. The remotest antiquity of the Indian era has always been a moot point among historians and other scholars. It is too lengthy in nature to be accepted by them open-heartedly. In fact, the authenticity of the longest ever era of the world has been fired on one ground or another. This system has also been challenged on the ground that it never got the sanction of people or never been in practice. This is why, while recounting Indian eras, the scholiasts often start from the Vikram era of 57 B.C. and fail to touch upon the original and actual system. Keeping in view all the pros and cons of the original Indian era christened as the Vedic era, we would like to observe as under:

(1) So far as its antiquity is concerned, it may appear hypothetical and fictitious to most historians and Indologists. On the other hand, geologists, anthropologists, biologists, physicists, and other scientists would speak highly of it, since their findings have led them to conclude

that the earth originated around 300-400 crore years ago and life flourished on it somewhere about 200-300 crore years ago.

Scientists have recently discovered that the existence of ancient microbial life on the red planet or Mars took place around 360 crore years ago. Their studies are based on intensive laboratory work for 10 years with sophisticated lasers and spectrometers on a piece of Martian meteorite weighing 1.9 Kg. found in Antarctica in 1984. Whatsoever be the reaction of scholars and scientists regarding this finding, one thing is clear that the sign of bacterial life appeared in our neighbourhood or on our planet around 3.5 billion years ago.

Recent research in genetic science have also proved that a Maithunī Sṛṣṭī (sexual production) had evolved on this earth some 200 to 300 crore years ago. If the existence of a Maithunī Sṛṣṭī could occur 200-300 crore years ago, there is a possibility that human life was also certainly in existence on the earth around 196 crore years ago.

Biologists like Lemark (1744-1829), William Smith (1769-1839), and Charles Darwin (1809-1882), etc also see the origin of biological life on the earth 100 to 150 crore years ago.

(2) So far as its sanction in the Indian society is concerned we find the mention of various phases of this era into the Vedic and the Paurāṇika sources. Besides, we have a Saṁkalpa tradition, which is as old as the Vedas themselves. This tradition has kept the year to year, month to month, day to day, even Muhurta (period of 48 minutes) to Muhurta record of the time that has elapsed since the inception of this era. The Saṁkalpa Pāṭhas from all over India have been gathered and on comparative examination, it has been found that there was strict uniformity so far as the reckonings of time are concerned except those of geographical references, which would have to differ naturally.

So far as the validity of its length is concerned, it may be maintained here that it was not a hypothetical reckoning of time-based on backward astronomical calculations. As per the Vedic and the Pauraṇika traditions, humans were present on the earth 196 crore years ago and the Vedas were composed and time reckoning was launched by the seers present then. The following geological, astronomical, biological and cultural codes of the Vedas stand to authenticate the very antiquity of the Indian era.

1. ***Parvata***— This is a well-established fact that the diction and style of a particular language are formed within a particular cultural background marked by the development of various sciences, moral ethos, and philosophy under various circumstances and as taken from various angles, a particular word may have various meanings. For instance, the term 'fire' in the sense of shooting came in vogue when the bombs were thrown at the enemy through canons by giving fire to the explosive material stored in its barrel. Now the use of this term has no longer remained relevant since we don't give fire for shooting bombs or bullets. But the same word is still in currency though the circumstances have changed and it is taken from a different angle. Similarly, under the circumstances created by the modern science, some new usages are in currency, e.g. 'He went there by air or by sea.' The above-given usages 'by air' or 'by sea' obviously implies to the aeroplane or ship. Suppose the modern science and its technology face an extinction due to some catastrophic reasons, and the above phrases are handed down to the future generations without the actual scientific background behind them. After a hundred years of a gap, these phrases would naturally appear to the then future generations a mere nonsense and nothing else. They would simply laugh at the currency of such foolish usages. Similar is the case with a number of Vedic usages, which have been handed down to us in their literal sense without any proper scientific or cultural background behind their evolution. Take for example the term 'parvata'. The very

term 'parvata' stands for mountains in the classical Sanskrit, but the same meaning doesn't hold good so far as the Vedas are concerned. In the Vedas, 'parvata' and all of its synonyms like 'adri' and 'giri' etc. refer to the clouds and boundary of the universe instead of earthly mountains. The ancient Vedic scholar Yāska (Kali era 2000-2100 or c 10th-11th century BC) has revealed this fact in his celebrated lexicon called the *Nighaṇṭu* (1.10). Several modern occidentals, as well as oriental scholars, wonder why Yāska has identified 'parvata' with the cloud. They, however, forget that it was not Yāṣka's personal view, but it was a long tradition handed down to Yāska that preserved the original geographical background within which the term *parvata* evolved. In fact, this great culture is not 3, 4, or 10 thousand years old but the chronology preserved by this culture since the time of its inception shows that it dates as early as 196 crores (1.9 Billion) years ago. The researches into geology have proved that there was a time when there were no mountains on the earth. The use of the term *parvata* in the sense of cloud in the Vedas clearly points out to the geographical scenario which prevailed during the time of their composition. This earth which is presently covered with mountain ranges was obviously devoid of any sort of mountain around 197 crore years. As per theories of orogeny, mountains appeared 60 crore years ago. Under the circumstances, it can unhesitatingly be inferred that the Vedic culture belonged to the period when the orogenic process had not started. This fact indirectly testifies to the authenticity and validity of the Indian era too. Since there were no mountains on the earth, in the beginning, the term 'parvata' or its synonyms like 'adri', 'grāvā', 'giri', etc. had nothing to do with mountains and so rather used sparingly to signify clouds.

Yāska observed in this connection as follows:

गिरिष्ठाः गिरिस्थायी गिरः पर्वतः। समुद्गगीर्णो भवति पर्ववान् पर्वतः पर्व पुनः पृणाते पृणन्ति तत् प्रकृतीतरत सन्धि सामान्यात् मेघस्थायी मेघोऽपि गिरिरेतस्मादेव।

giriṣṭhā girishāyī giriḥ parvataḥ samudgīrṇo bhavati parvavān parvataḥ parva punaḥ pṛṇāteḥ prīṇantiti tat prakrtītarat sandhi sāmānyāt meghasthāyī megho'pi giriretasmādeva. Nir. 1.20.

'Giri' is known as 'parvata', since it is the vomited vapour of the earth. It is so-called as it is constituted of fragments. It is so-called as it brings up the living beings on the earth with water, etc. These qualities are discernible in clouds. Hence clouds are called 'giri'.

Later on, these qualities were also found associated with the mountain ranges that emerged on the earth and so the term 'parvata' and its synonyms were also begun to be applied to the mountains and de grado en grado this term got conventionalized for mountains only. This is why Lord Macaulay (1800-1859) laughs at the mention of 'parvata' flying in the sky. Had he been well conversed with Vedic dicta he wouldn't have laughed, rather would have enjoyed the Vedic wisdom.

2. **Nadī**, **Sindhu**, **Samudra**: In the Vedas, we have references of 'nadi' and 'sindhu' being used for rainy waters and water flowing on the earth respectively.

Thus applications of the terms 'nadī' and 'sindhu' respectively in the sense of rainy waters and rivers shows that Vedic culture flourished by the period when oceans were not formed on the earth and the rivers were in the process of formation. Due to the non-formation of oceanic waters by the time of evolution of this culture, the terms 'samudra' and 'arṇava' were also used to denote mid-sphere rather than terrestrial oceans. As per researches in Geology, the ancient most mountains and the oceans were formed on the earth in the pre-Cambrian or Algonican era i.e. between 250 to 60 crores of years ago. The Vedic culture which has recorded its history since 197 crore years ago clearly reveals that the oceans and mountains were formed on this earth within the range of 197 crore years. In fact, the Vedic litanies were composed when there were no mountain and ocean visibly appeared on the earth and the rivers were under the process of formation.

3. **Sarasvatī**: Sarasvatī was the name of the first river system that originated on the earth. The very first appearance of this river system on the earth owes to the clouds. The most celebrated Ṛgvedic seer Vasiṣṭha had clearly observed its origin from the celestial parvatas i.e. clouds. According to him:

आ नो दिवो बृहतः पर्वतादा सरस्वती यजता गन्तु

यज्ञु हवं देवी जुजुषाणा घृताची शग्मो नो वाचमुशती श्रृणोतु।

ā no divo bṛhataḥ parvatādā sarasvatī yajatā gantu Yajñam havaṁ devī jujuṣāṇā ghṛtācī śagmo no vācamuśatī śṛṇotu

'From the great celestial parvatas (clouds) Sarasvatī flows towards the site of Yajña. It hears the voice of a person who offers the oblation of ghṛta with the desire of receiving it.'

Parvata here clearly refers to a cloud and not to a mountain as is conventionally held. The attributive 'divaḥ' (celestial) bears out the hypothesis that parvata was only intended for clouds and not for mountains, as there can be no mountain in the sky except clouds.

Not only Vasiṣṭha, but another seer had it the same way. According to him, the Sarasvatī is the only flow of waters on earth that issues from the giris (clouds).

ऐका चेतत् सरस्वती नदीनाम् शुचिर्यति गिरिभ्यः समुद्रात्।

ekā cetat sarasvatī nadinām śuciryatī giribhyaḥ ā samudrāt (*RV.* 7.95.2).

The concept of the first origin of the Sarasvatī from clouds also shows that the Vedas were composed at the time when there was no mountain, no glacier on the earth. It marks the period before the origin of glaciers on this part of the earth. Geologist has traced the appearance of the glaciation on this part of the Globe in the Triassic period i.e. around 22 crore years ago. So there is nothing wrong if we infer that the Vedic hymns containing the description of the origin of rivers from clouds were composed before glaciation.

This fact also bears the testimony to the authenticity of the Indian era.

4. **Brahmaputra**: the Vedas don't have any mention of the Brahmaputra. In fact, the Brahmaputra is the creation of the Himalayan mountains. When there were no Himalayan ranges, there was no Brahmaputra. The Pauraṇika (*Vāyu* and *Matsya*) traditions describe the origin of the Brahmaputra from the lake of Hemasṛṅga. Similarly, the Sarasvatī and Jyotiṣmatī have also been described to have their origins from the lakes of Hemasṛṅga. Hemasṛṅga reminds us of the glaciation around Mānasasara. It was the upliftment of the Himalayan ranges that caused the Brahmaputra severed from that of Sarasvatī. The records of the *Vāyu* and the *Matsya Purāṇas* belonging to the period of origin of the Himalayan ranges of mountains containing the description of Lohita river or the Brahmaputra rising from the lohita lake situated at the foot of Lohita Hemsṛṅga (*Vāyu*) and Sarvoṣadha *(Matsya Purāṇa).* The absence of the Brahmaputra in the Vedas also proves the Vedas older than the Himalayas and so the antiquity of the Indian era.

5. **Himvat**: A few references in the Vedas (*RV.* 10.121.4) of *Himvat* shows the presence of glaciated regions in the Vedic period. The word Himalaya today is taken to mean the Himalayan ranges of mountains. But the main thing to note is that Himalaya is a term of quite a later period. In its earlier references ranging from the Vedas to the Epics and the *Puraṇas,* the term used was 'himvat' which literally means 'a place of snow' or 'glaciated region'. Moreover, the later evolved term Himalaya also doesn't indicate any sort of hill or mountain rather it also, in its literal sense, points to the glaciated region or the home of snow. In fact, the term 'hima' never denoted hilly

terrain, rather it denoted glaciers. Since the later originated mountains also become the abode of the glaciers, then they came to be called the Himalaya mountains which literally means abode of glaciers. The Purāṇic tradition narrates the origin of the rivers of the North India like Ganga, Sarasvatī, Gaṇḍaka, Yamuna, Sindhu, Sutlej, Chenab, Devikā, Kuhu, Gomatī, etc. from the foot of glaciers.

himvatpādanissṛtā (*Brahma Purāṇa* 2.16.27)

Such references are clear-cut records of the geological scenario of glaciation in the Triassic period i.e. 22 crores of years ago.

6. **Four Seas:** Some of the Vedic ṛcās seems to be composed after the formation of seas or oceans took place. Such ṛcās shed an ample good light in the presence of the seas on the earth. In the chain of such ṛcas, we meet with some as describe the presence of four seas, one each in four directions of the Indian subcontinent, e.g.

रायः समुद्रांश्चतुरोऽस्मभ्यं सोम विश्वतः ।

rāyaḥ samudrāṁścaturo'smabhyaṁ soma viśvataḥ.

(*RV.* 9.33.6.)

See also:

स्वायुधं स्ववसं सुनीथं चतुःसमुद्रं धरूणं रयीणाम् ।

svāyudhaṁ svavasaṁ sunīthaṁ catuḥsamudraṁ dharuṇaṁ rayīṇām. (*RV.* 10.47.2.)

The period when this country was bounded by four seas, goes back to 10 crore years ago.

The palaeomagnetism of oceanic rocks indicates that the continents started separating during the last 10 crore years. Near the end of the Carboniferous and the beginning of the Permian (i.e. 30 crore years ago), the landmasses were assembled into two supercontinents Gondwana in the south and Laurasia in the north (Enayat Ahmed, 1993:80).

This assemblage of two supercontinents persisted till

about 15 crore years ago, but the continents were discernible from their outlines. By about 10 crore years ago, the expansion of the Indian ocean by further separation of Antarctica from South Africa and South America and drifting of India and Australia became more prominent than the Atlantic which still remained as a relatively narrow ocean particularly in the north. The picture given below displays the portion of the Indian sub-continent and the seas surrounding it in the four directions.

Map of Eocene Period

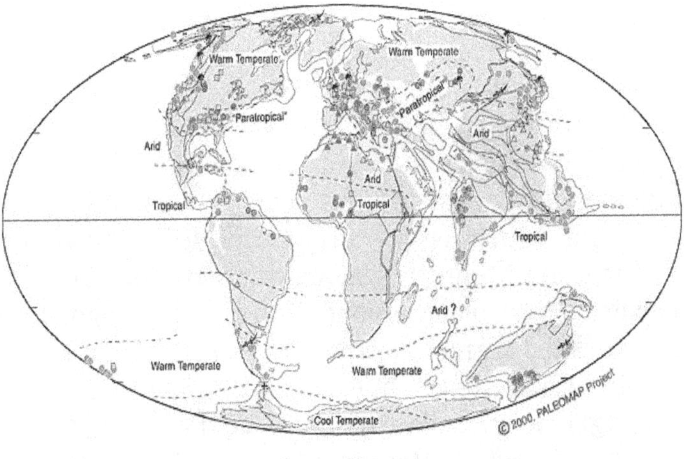

Lower Eocene

Thus from the above geological description, it is crystal clear that India was surrounded by four seas mentioned in the ṛcas of the Ṛgveda composed around 10 crore years ago. This marks evidently the pre-Himalayan period.

7. **Triviṣṭapa**: According to the Paurāṇika tradition, Humans originated first in the area of Triviṣṭapa (Tibet).

त्रिविष्टपे जाता सृष्टिः ।

triviṣṭape jātā sṛṣṭiḥ.

In the Paurāṇic and Epic traditions Triviṣṭapa has been remembered as a place where from devas descended first.

It is often known as svarloka being the highest plateau on the earth. Triviṣṭapa being Tibet in its corrupt form. According to Geologists, Tibet formed as an offshore region of the Gondwana land during the Palaeozoic era. (Enayat Ahmed, 1993: 94)

Palaeozoic era makes its beginning as early as 60 crore years ago and ends as late as 27 crore years ago. So Triviṣṭap's mention as a cradle of deva sṛṣṭi at the beginning of the creation of human beings forces one to accept the great culture as old as the formation of Tibet itself.

8. **Vaḍvāgni:** As per modern geological researches, the Himalayan ranges of mountains started to form in the Eocene period, i.e. around 7 crore years ago. It is also a proven fact that the Himalayan ranges of the mountains formed from volcanoes. Here it may be pointed out that age-old Paurāṇika traditions have reported the submarine volcanic activities in the name of the Vaḍvāgni. The vaḍvāgni which is literally meant for submarine fire is nothing else, but the submarine volcanic activities that began to take place around 7 crore years ago, if geology provides the correct information. The tradition of the *Skand Purāṇa* (7.33.40-41) holds that the Sarasvatī drained the vaḍvāgni to the western sea at Prabhāsa Pāṭan. This traditional record of the *Skanda Purāṇa* obviously points out to 7 crore-year-old submarine volcanic activities that gave rise to the Himalayan mountains. Due to volcanic activities at the submarine level of Manas sara, the submarine surface of Manas sara, or Tethys sea as it is called today, began to uplift and the outflow of water due to the uplifted submarine surface of Manas sara began to be drained by a river channel called Sarasvatī towards the western sea at Prabhāsa Pāṭan in the modern Gujarat state. The drainage of submarine volcanic eruptions by Sarasvatī has also been attested in the tradition of several other *Purāṇas*. Special mention in this connection may be made of the *Padma Purāṇa* (5.18.154-160).

The record of volcanic activities at the submarine surface level of Tethys sea clearly proves the Vedic culture older than the Himalayas.

9. **Saṅkalpa Pāṭha:** The Saṅkalpa tradition that has been handed down to us reads a phrase as under.

मेरोर्दक्षिणभागे जम्बुद्वीपे भारतवर्षे भरतखण्डे

merordakṣiṇa bhāge jambudvīpe bhāratavaıṣe, bharatakhaṇḍe

The Saṅkalpā Pāṭha indicates that Jambudvīpa, Bhāratavarṣa and Bharatakhaṇḍa are located in the southern hemisphere of the Meru. Before discussing the above statement, it is necessary to know about Meru and its southern point. Meru was the name of the lithosphere with two polar caps. This fact has been corroborated by the *Yogavāsıṣṭha.* Accordingly, *Meru* is the name of the surface of the earth.

meru bhūpıṣṭhaḥ (*Yogavāsıṣṭha,* 59.27)

In fact, the word 'Maru' is the actual representative of the Meru. 'Maru' is also indicative of a sandy desert devoid of water. This meru had two polar caps and so divided into two halves. The upper half is the northern hemisphere and the lower half is the southern hemisphere. Now, one will be able to comprehend the Saṅkalpa pāṭha. Accordingly, Jaṁbudvīpa in which are located Bhāratavarṣ a and Bharatakhaṇḍa was situated in the southern hemisphere of the Meru.

Here it can easily be inferred that when the extant Saṅkalpa pāṭha was introduced, the Indian subcontinent was towards the south pole. In the present circumstances, when we have drifted towards 7^0 north, it is very difficult to make out the actual significance of the extant Saṅkalpa pāṭha. Its actual intent can only be understood when one looks back the geographical conditions, as gathered from the theories of drifters like Wegener, etc., when the Indian subcontinent was the part of the southern hemisphere around 35 crore years ago or at the end of the Carboniferous period of the Palaeozoic era.

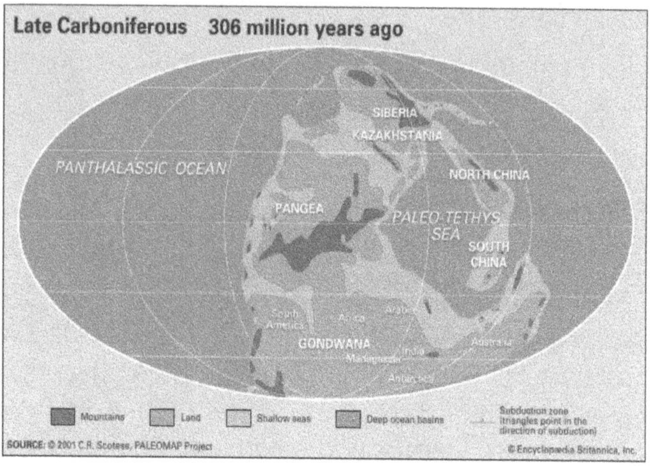

The researches in geology have shown alarming results regarding the drift in the location of different regions of the globe. Accordingly, the Indian subcontinent continued to be the part of the southern hemisphere until the early Pleistocene period of a Neozoic era or Quaternary era, i.e. till 10 lakh years ago when this continent drifted right on the equatorial point.

10. **Location of the Kailāsa**: The drift in the geographical location of the Indian subcontinent has also been suggested by the Paurāṇika records of the Perennial era. Accordingly, the location of the Kailaśa mountain was earlier in the south, but it was shaken by the kick of Śiva during his Taṇḍava Nṛtya and transferred towards the north. (Dr. Padmachandra Kashyapa, *Bhārata darśana mālā*, 6)

Here Tāṇḍava Nṛtya of Śiva signifies the forces of drift or plate-tectonic activities that changed the position of the Kailāsa mountain from south to north. One may remember well that the Himalayan ranges of mountains began to form as early as 7 crore years ago, as per modern estimates and 12 crore years ago as per ancient Indian view, and the Śivālaka ranges of mountains were formed as the result of the last stages of the upliftment of the Himalayan ranges ranging from 1 crore year ago to 20 lakh years ago. We are very much aware of the fact that 20 lakh years ago, i.e. by the period of completion of the Himalayan ranges and the Śivālaka ranges we were very much around 7^0 south of the equator. Presently we have drifted towards 7^0 north of the equator.

The concept of drifting continents or plate tectonics of the earth has also been suggested in the methods of the construction of Vedic fire altars. According to the *Brāhmaṇas*, fire-altar represented the earth. The *Taittirīya Saṁhitā.* (2.6.4) has clarified this fact as:

ऐतावती वै पृथिवी यावती वै वेदी।

etāvatī vai pṛthivī yāvatī vedī

'Fire altar has the same parameters as that of the earth.' So, construction of the *Vedī* also symbolises the formation of the earth. Altar construction has been marked with two specific movements. One is 'udakkrama', i.e, the movement towards the north and another is 'prākkrama', i.e. the movement towards east. Thus, in the construction of the Vedī, the drift of its continents is suggested.

11. **The Vaivasvata Manvantara**: As per *Avanti Sundari Kāthā,* the Vaivasvata Manu resided at Sthāneśvara, a place close to Modern Kurukshetra and well known by the name Thāṇesara. The *Ṛgveda* egisters a Mantra written by Kaśyapa Mārīca, a seer of Vaivasvata era or *(Manvantara)* which reads as follows:

यत्र राजा वैवस्वतो यत्रावरोधनं दिवः।

यत्र मूर्यह्वतीर् आपस्तत्र माममृतं कृधीन्द्रायेन्दो परिश्रवः।

yatra rājā vaivasvato yatrāvarodhanaṁ divaḥ
yatrā mūryahvatīr āpastatra māmamṛtaṁ kṛdhīndrāyendo pari srava.

'Where there is Vivasvān's son is the king, where there flow big-big rivers, and where there lies the door towards the dyuloka, there immortalise me.'

The historical tradition of the *Vāyu Purāṇa* (50.88) also records the location of the Vaivasvata as under:

दक्षिणेन पुनर्मेरो मानसस्य च मूर्धनि।

वैवस्वतो निवसति यमः यमने पुरे।।

dakṣiṇena punar mero mānasasya ca mūrdhani
vaivasvato nivasati yamaḥ yamane pure

'That is to say, in the southern hemisphere of the Meru, and the upper region of the Manas sara i.e. Tethys sea resides Vivasvān's son, in the down south in the Yamanapura.'

The references of the *RV.* and the *Vāyupurāṇa* alarmingly disclose the fact that the Mantras of the *RV.* were visualised when the Indian subcontinent used to be in the southern hemisphere and the south pole was endowed with north polarity. Here it may be pointed out that the Vaivasvata Manvantara commenced 13 crore years ago or say in the Cretaceous period of the Mesozoic era by the time the Indian subcontinent used to be around 30^0 south of the equator. The Paurāṇika memoirs and geographical history of the earth have an alarming similarity. From the above discussion, one wouldn't hesitate to infer that the Vedic culture was fairly old, older than even the mighty Himalayas.

12. **Fishes and Frogs:** Fishes and frogs find a significant place in the Vedas. There are separate hymns devoted to fishes and frogs. The geological history of the earth tells us that fishes and frogs had originated on the earth some 40 crore years ago, i.e. in a Devonian period of the palaeozoic era. In addition Horse, Cow, Crocodiles and Tortoises also find a significant mention in the Vedic literature. These animals are also considered to have been born on the earth around 7 crore years ago. A fossil of dinosaur's skin, which feels like a thick bicycle tire-rough and bumpy, with somewhat symmetrical clumps of little

crimped-edged knobs, discovered by a graduate student near Deming in Southern New Mexico dates the existence of massive beasts back to 70 million years ago. This biological code supported by geological and archaeological findings also proves the Vedas to be fairly old.

13. **Cultural Code:** As the cultural tradition had it, Indians used to call their nation or geographically bounded country as motherland, e.g. we call our country Bhārata as Bhārata mātā. The concept of motherhood is associated with the country because the concept of birth is associated with the country as closely as it is with the mother. Just as a mother is the birth giver, similarly a country is also a birthplace. Hence it is always attributed to the mother and the country of the birth. The study of the Vedas tells us that no country or geographical area in original hymns of the Vedas has been mentioned as a mother, rather earth itself has been found endowed with such attributive as mother—

भूमि माता पुत्रोऽहं पृथिव्याः ।।

Bhūmī mātā putro'ham pṛthivyāḥ (*A V. Bhumi Sūkta*)

'Earth is my mother and I am the child of earth.'

The association of motherhood with the earth simply reveals the fact that this culture is fairly old and belongs to the period when the earth was practically one super-continent and had not fractured into various continents. This geological situation persisted till the period of palaeozoic era or 60 crore years. In fact, the origin of the Indian subcontinent as a separate landmass took place by the end of a Carboniferous era or 35 crore years ago when it was situated between 30^0 south of the equator. See the map of the end of the Carboniferous era as given above.

So this cultural code also supports the author's hypothesis that Vedic culture and the Vedic era was undoubtedly 197 crore (1.9 billion) years old.

14. **Astronomical evidence**: Above cited geological code of the Vedas and Indian chronology of 197 crore

years is also supported by astronomical evidence of two kinds.

1. Firstly we find the important role of the Aśvinīkumaras (The two bright stars Alpha and Beta Aries) in the *RV.* They have been praised in 53 hymns.

To sum up, it can be inferred from the above evidence that the composition of the Ṛgvedic verses took place during the period of the Aśvinī calendar or during the period when the year started when the sun was near the Aśvinī Nakṣatra (or Alpha and Beta Arietis).

In the *VS* (31.22) also it is clearly stated that *Aśvinī* was the mouth of the present creation (*aśvinau vyāttam*). All this points out that the beginning of Indian chronology 197294996 years ago took place in the Aśvinī Nakṣatra. Keeping in view of this historical fact, Indian Scholiast made the Aśvinī Nakṣatra as the basis of their chronology. *Aśvinī* calendar of the Ṛgvedic period also proves the fact that the Vedas were visualised 1.9 billion years ago by the high-spirited seers present at that period.

2. Apart from the above evidence, the second evidence is quite revealing. Accordingly, the year in the Ṛgvedic period contained 360 days or 720 pairs of *Ahas* (days) and *Rātris* (night). This fact has clearly been recorded in the verses of the *RV.* as under:

द्वादशारं नहि तज्जराय वर्वर्ति चक्रं परि द्यामृतस्य।

आ पुत्राग्ने मिथुनासो अत्र सप्त शतानि विंशतिश्च तस्थुः।।

dvādaśāraṁ na hi tajjarāya varvarti cakraṁ pari dyāmṛtasya. ā putrā agne mithunāso atra sapta śatānivimśatiśca tasthuḥ. (*RV.* 1.164.2)

'The wheel (of time) having twelve spokes (months) revolves around the heavens, but it doesn't wear out. O Agni! 720 pairs of sons (ahorātras) ride this wheel.'

द्वादश प्रधयश्चक्रमेकं त्रिणि नाभ्यानि क उताच्चिकेत

तस्मिन्तशाकं त्रिशता न शंकवोऽर्पिताः षष्टिर्न चलाचलासः।।

dvādaśa pradhayaścakramekaṁ trīṇi nābhyāni ka ut acciketa tasmintsākaṁ triśatā na śaṅkavo'rpitāḥ ṣaṣṭirna calācalāsaḥ.

'Twelve spokes (months), one wheel (year) three navels (seasons): who understands these? In these, there are installed 360 śaṅkus (rods, i.e. days) like pegs which do not loosen.'

The tradition of the *Tait. Br.* (7.17) also remembers the relic of this ancient most historical fact of astronomy as follows:

त्रीणि च वै शतानि षष्टिश्च संवत्सरस्याहनि सप्त च वै शतानि विंशतिश्च संवत्सरस्याहोरात्रयः।

trīṇi ca vai śatāni ṣaṣṭiśca saṁvatsarasyāhāni sapta ca vai śatāni viṁśatiśca saṁvatsarasyāhorātrayaḥ.

'A year has 360 days, and 720 days and nights together.'

Thus a year of 360 days consisting of 12 months of 30 days each formed the earliest astronomical phenomenon and thereby the earliest Vedic calendar, as is evident from the above-cited references. It may here be informed that the month was also further divided into five *Ṣaḍahas* of 6 days each.

The year of 360 days was not an approximation or presented a vague idea of the measurement of days in a year. It was rather a concrete measurement of the days of a year. In fact, the above-cited concept may be seen in the light of the theories of expanding the universe. The Vedic seers have already expounded this theory. According to them the origin of space or *antarikṣa* is the result of the separation of planets from stars. Earlier they were together, and so there was no space between them. With the passage of time due to sliding apart of planets and stars, space between them became visible. Since the space between them became visible, it was known as *antarikṣa.* For instance the *Ś.Br.* (Author, 1995:16) had it as:

> 'In the beginning stars and planets were together. In the process of evolution, both began to recede and the space between them became visible. Because space became visible, it was called *antarikṣa*'

Modern astrophysicists have also come to nonetheless similar conclusions. According to them, crores of years ago nebulas were close to each other. Even the moon is also going away from the earth, day by day and year by year. It has been calculated that the distance between the moon and the earth is increasing by 13 cms. per year. Similarly, the distance between the earth and the sun is also increasing. Now the earth is 149597870.6 crore Kms. away from the sun. It is revolving around the sun on its ecliptic path of 149597870.6x2x22/7 = 940329472.34 crore Kms. @ 107270 kms. per hour. Imagine the time when the earth was closer to the sun. Its distance being short, the ecliptic path was also short. Under the circumstances, the earth was capable of revolving around the Sun in a shorter period than what it is now. In fact, 197 crore years ago the earth revolved around the sun in 360 days only, so the year was also described as consisting of 360 days. This shows that the ecliptic path of the earth was 107270x8640 (360 days) hrs= 926812800 kms long 1970000000 years if the period of the rate of revolution of the earth remains unchanged. This will make the distance of the earth from the sun 926812800x7÷2÷22= 147447490 kms before 197 crore years ago. So there is a total increase of distance of the earth from sun 149597870 kms (present) - 147447490 (1970000000 years ago)= 2150379 kms. This makes an average increase of the distance between earth and sun 215037900000÷1970000000 =109 cms per year in 1970000000 years. Presently this increase is being calculated @ 15 cms per year. It shows that in the beginning, the rate of increase of distance was much higher than the present one.

Keeping in view the importance of 360, the Indian astronomers fixed 360 days for the calendric year. Later on, to record any sort of increase in the revolution period due to an increase in the distance between the earth and the sun, the provision of the intercalary period was made to be added to the actual period of 360 days. Thus the beginning of the year in the Aśvinī constellations and number of 360 days in a year in the Ṛgvedic period support the above hypothesis.

All the above-cited evidence but indicate the presence of humans on the earth crores of years ago, thereby leading one to infer that the Vedic era was launched by the seers present 197 crore years ago and was recollected safely and carefully by a long uninterrupted tradition of Saṁkalpa Pāṭhas.

Following the lines of arguments cited above, it can further be observed that the Vedas were visualised somewhere near the inception of the Indian chronology. The internal evidence of the Vedas based on the linguistic analysis undoubtedly proves this fact. Though for the time being scholars may have their reservations on this contentious issue, since they may raise questions as to how a memory of such a long period was retained in the Vedic and the Pauranika tradition. It may not seem feasible, but it may also not be impossible. The manner in which the long uninterrupted tradition has been safeguarded is unparalleled in the history of humankind. Further investigations in various fields of science will be able to shed ample good light on the authenticity of the Indian traditional viewpoint.

Let me conclude that only the traditional viewpoint is acceptable and any inference drawn on the basis of some fragmentary references of traditional view would only be misleading and dangerous.

Recensions/Schools (Śākhās) of the Vedas

A great deal of effort was made in preserving the Vedas in their original form. In the beginning, the Vedas were passed on from one generation to another orally, but being a vast body of literature very minor changes crept in the oral tradition handled by different teachers from time to time. This gave rise to the origin of different schools of the Vedas, which are very much similar to each other. These schools vary sometimes in the pronunciation of words or sometimes have words replaced by other words with similar meaning or different meanings and the scientific truth revealed in the Mantra or the subject matter of the Mantra.

To illustrate it, I can quote some examples from the *Sāmaveda.* When Mantras in the *Sāmaveda* were borrowed from the *Ṛgveda* in order to set them to the tune of cosmic music some 106 of the Mantras registered variations, some significant and others insignificant. Some of the variations occurred due to the musical exigencies, but most of them have occurred due to the articulatory factors such as slip of tongue, etc When the Ṛgvedic passages are compared with the corresponding passages from the *Sāmaveda,* the following types of variations come to the notice.

1. **Semantic variations:** We may find variations where intent of the respective stanzas have been affected, e.g.

समिदन्य इळते *Samidanya* ***ilate*** *RV.*1.36.1

समिदन्य इन्धते *Samidanya* ***indhate*** *SV.* 59

In the above-cited illustrations, we find that the Ṛgvedic इळते *Ilate* (to praise) has changed in the *Sāmaveda* into इन्धते *indhate* (to burn). As such here the variation has affected the semantic element (meaning).

2. **Phonetic variations:** In some of the variations we

come across interchange of sounds. For instance, the Ṛgvedic labial sounds have interchanged into labio-dental sounds in the *Sāmaveda*, such as पृष्टिं दिवः *pṛṣṭiṁ divaḥ* (*RV.* 9.39.2) becomes वृष्टिं दिवः *vṛṣṭim divaḥ* (*SV.* 899) where the Rigvedic 'p' sound changes into 'v' in the *Sāmaveda.*

3. Ellison of sounds: We also come across cases where some sounds of the *Ṛgveda* have been dropped in the *Sāmaveda*, e.g. स्तोमा *stomā* of the *RV.* 8.5.3.1 becomes सोम *soma* in the *Sāmaveda* (194).

4. Metathesis: We also met with a case of metathesis of sounds, e.g. अरिर *arira* of the *Ṛgveda* 8.2.14 becomes रयिर *rayira* in the *Sāmaveda* where 'a' and 'r' sounds are metamorphosed.

5. Anaptyxis: We may also find Anapycal tendencies, e.g अप्या *apyā* of the *RV.* 9.108.6 becomes अपि या *api yā* in the *Sāmaveda* (585) with the insertion of vowel sound 'i' between two consonant sounds 'p' and 'y'.

In addition to this, we may also find morphological variations, like variations in nominal stems, in personal endings, in case of endings, in participle stems, in number markers, in gender markers, in attributives, in nouns, moods, etc. Even syntactical variations are also visible here and there. I don't want to divulge into details, as this is not an appropriate place to deal with them. These examples are sufficient to understand the trend.

The Mantras of the four different Vedas were preserved orally by various disciples of the one and the same Guru giving rise to various Guru-Śiṣya traditions. When the Mantras passed from one generation to another orally in different Guru-Śiṣya traditions, the above types of variations occurred leading to the origin of various recensions or śākhās of the Vedas. Thus various śākhās or schools of the Vedas represented various Guru-Śiṣya traditions of the Vedas. We come across multiple recensions of each of the four the Vedas. For instance,

According to the *Muktikopnishad*, the *Ṛgveda* had 21 recensions, the *Yajurveda* had 109 recensions, the *Sāmaveda* had 1,000 and the *Atharvaveda* had 50 branches, having a total of approximately 100,000 verses in their 1,180 branches. Nowadays only 20,379 verses are available. Of the total, 10,552 verses belong to the *Ṛgveda* (arranged in 10 sections called *maṇḍalas*), 1,975 verses belong to the *Yajurveda* (in 40 chapters), 1,875 verses belong to the *Sāmaveda* (in 21 chapters) and 5,977 verses belong to the *Atharvaveda* (in 20 chapters). Some of these texts have survived, the most have lost or yet to be traced.

The traditional source of information on the Śākhas of the each Veda is the *Caraṇa-vyūha*, of which two, mostly similar, versions exist: the 49th *pariśiṣṭa* of the *Atharvaveda*, ascribed to Śaunaka, and the 5th *pariśiṣṭa* of the Śukla (White) *Yajurveda*, ascribed to Kātyāyana. These have a list of the recensions that were believed to have once existed as well as those still extant at the time these works were compiled. Today only a small number of recensions have survived. Hereunder we shall give a detailed description of various recensions of the four Vedas along with their Saṁhitas, Brāhamaṇa texts, Ārṇyaka Texts, and Upaniṣads.

Here it may also be clarified that the Saṁhitas are a compilation of the Mantra portion of the Vedas. The Mantra is the knowledge of creation seen or visualised by seers in their Samādhi. The Brāhmaṇas are the explanatory portion of the Vedas. In the Brāhmaṇas, the subject matter contained in the Mantras of the concerned Vedas is explained. This explanation is generally associated with the physical, astrophysical, and metaphysical part of the process of creation or say the evolution of the cosmos as it has happened.

The Āraṇyakas deal with the human beings' preparedness on the journey of spirituality and the Upaniṣads deal with the journey to the path of mokṣa or realisation of Brahman.

The Ṛgveda

Saṁhita Texts: According to Śaunaka's *Caraṇa-vyūha* there are five śākhā-s of the *Ṛgveda.* They are named as

1. **Śākala**: This Śākhā is extant today. Śākala śākhā of the *Ṛgveda* belongs to the region of Videha, in modern north Bihar, south of Nepal.

2. **Bāṣkala:** This Śākhā is also extant today. The Bāṣkala recension of the *Ṛgveda* has the Khila Pāṭha which is not present in the Śākala text but is preserved in one Kashmir manuscript (now at Pune).

3. **Aśvalāyana**: Only a few Mantras are extant

4. **Śāṅkhāyana**: Not extant

5. **Māṇḍukāyana**: Not extant.

Brāhmaṇa Texts: The *Aitareya Brāhmaṇa*, the *Kauṣitakī Brāhmaṇa* (*Śāṅkhāyana Brāhmaṇa*)

Āraṇyaka Texts: The *Aitareya Āraṇyaka*

Upaniṣads: The *Aitareya Upaniṣad*

The Yajurveda

Śaunaka's *Caraṇa-vyūha* lists forty-two or forty-four out of eighty-six śache-s of the *Yajurveda*, but that only five of these are now extant, and a sixth is partially extant. These are the *Vājasaneyī* or the *Mādhyandina*, the *Kāṇva*; the *Taittirīya*, the *Maitrāyaṇī*, the *Kaṭha*, and the *Kapiṣṭhala*.

The Śākhās of the *Yajurveda* are divided in the Śukla (lit. meaning white) and the Kṛṣṇa (lit. meaning black) schools. The Śukla recensions have separate Brāhmaṇa texts, while the Kṛṣṇa ones have their own Brāhmaṇa texts interspersed between the Mantras. Following are the names of the various Saṁhitas, Brāhmaṇas, Āraṇyakas, and Upaniṣads belonging to the

Śukla and the *Kṛṣṇa Yajurveda.*

1- The Śukla Yajurveda

Saṁhita Texts: 1. The Mādhyandina Saṁhitā: recited all over North India.

2. The Vājasaneyī Samhita Kāṇva: Recited in Odisha and Karnataka.

Brāhmaṇa Texts: The Śatapatha Brāhmaṇa.

Āraṇyaka Texts: Part of the Śatapatha Brāhmaṇa (14.1-8).

Upaniṣads: The *Bṛhadāraṇyaka Upaniṣad* (part of the *Śatapatha Brāhmaṇa* 14.3-8), the *Iśāvāsya Upaniṣad* (40th Chapter of the *Yajurveda*).

3. The *Kṛṣṇa Yajurveda*

Saṁhitā texts: 1. The Taittirīya Saṁhitā: Recited all over south India and Konkan;

2. The *Maitrāyaṇī Saṁhitā*: Recited in Nasik, Maharashtra.

3. The *Kaṭha Saṁhitā* (KS)

4. The *Kapiṣṭhala-Kaṭha and*

5. The *Kāṭhaka Saṁhitā.*

Brāhmaṇa texts: The *Taittirīya Brāhmaṇa*, the *Vādhūla Brāhmaṇa.*

Āraṇyaka Texts: the *Taittirīya Āraṇyaka*, the *Kaṭha Āraṇyaka.*

Upaniṣads: The *Taittirīya Upaniṣad*, the *Maitrāyaṇī*, the *Śvetāśvatara* and the *Kaṭha Upaniṣad.*

The Sāmaveda

Out of 1000 recensions, only the following are known and extant ones.

Saṁhita texts: 1. The *Kauthumīya Saṁhitā*: Recited all over North and South India.

2. The *Rāṇāyaṇīya Saṁhitā*: Recited by Gokarṇa and Deśastha Brahmins.

3. The *Jaiminīya/Talvakāra Saṁhitā*: Recited by Nambudris and Cholliyal of Tamilnadu.

4. The *Śāṭyāyana Saṁhitā*: Not extant.

Brāhmaṇa texts: The *Jaiminīya*, the *Āṛṣeya*, the *Talvakāra*, the *Jaiminīya Upaniṣad Brāhmaṇa*, the *Pañcaviṁśa Brāhmaṇa*

Āraṇyaka Texts: The *Talvakāra Āraṇyaka*

Upaniṣads: The *Chāndogya Upaniṣad*, The *Kena Upaniṣad*

The Atharvaveda

Saṁhitā texts: 1. The *Śaunaka Saṁhitā*: Recited all over North and South India. The *Śaunaka* is the only śākhā of the *Atharvaveda* for which both printed texts and an active oral tradition are known to still exist.

2. *Paippalāda Saṁhitā*: The *Paippalāda tradition* was discontinued, and its text is known only from manuscripts collected since the 20th century. However, some Odisha Brahmins still continue the tradition of *Paippalāda.*

Brāhmaṇa texts: the *Gopatha Brāhmaṇa*

Upaniṣads: the *Muṇḍaka*, the *Praśna Upaniṣad*

Rules of Interpretations

The language that we speak consists of words and their meaning. The word is 'body', of a language and the meaning, in fact, is the 'soul'.

One single word may have different meanings when spoken by different persons in different contexts.

The first meaning is known as abhidā, i.e. the apparent meaning. The apparent meaning is the popular meaning known to everybody by way of convention. It may also be defined as conventional or literal meaning. Apart from apparent meaning, the second one is known as the intended meaning. Intended meaning reflects the intention of the speaker. A speaker may not intend to speak in the conventional sense. As such intended meaning may differ from the apparent or popular meaning. In his idiosyncratic way, a speaker may intend to use the same words in some other extended or implied (suggested) meanings.

Thus intended meaning may be classified into two types.

Extended meaning: Intended meaning of the speaker may reflect the extended meaning in a figurative or metaphoric sense. For example, the word 'Agni' stands for a fire in a conventional or apparent or popular sense. But the speaker may extend the meaning of 'Agni' in his idiosyncratic language for the other things also that symbolise 'Agni' in their characteristics. For instance, the things that symbolise 'Agni' in its characteristics are the sun, the stars, the energy, the electricity, the digestive fire, the fire of conflagration, the (fire of) anger, the charging, the (fire of) knowledge, teacher, saint, commander, king, head of the institution, anger, and God. So they may also be referred to as 'Agni'. To find out the extended sense we shall have to depend upon the etymology of the words. The extended meaning may also be further divided into two types. a). Primary meaning and b). Secondary meaning.

The primary meaning is the main extended meaning and others are secondary meanings. In the context of the Vedas, spiritual meaning is the primary meaning and social, astrophysical, or physical meanings are the secondary meanings. In the Vedic tradition, there is a dictum *परोक्षप्रिया इव हि देवाः प्रत्यक्ष द्विषः। Prokṣapriyā iva hi devāḥ pratyakṣa dvıṣaḥ.* (The Vedic seers intend or love to explain mysteries in the extended or suggested meanings and not in apparent meaning.' So whatever seems the apparent meaning of the words or the acts in the Vedas that is not the true meaning, but whatever extended sense is deduced with the help etymology according to the context may be the real meaning of the Vedas. Since the Vedas consists of the eternal laws or knowledge of creation emanating from Brahman, their meanings have to be extended or suggested ones, since they are to define the whole creation with one law called as 'ṛta'. There cannot be two or more laws to define the different parts. If there is one law defining one segment of creation and another law defining the other segment, that cannot be a true law. If the Newtonian law of gravitation defines only the gravitation power of heavenly bodies, it cannot be an ultimate law as per Vedic system. The attraction/gravitation not only exists between heavenly bodies but between every two things born in this world. The phenomenon of attraction/gravitation is registered at the metaphysical level, biological level, astrophysical level, and physical level, the ultimate law will define all types of attraction/gravitation existing at various levels of creation. The law of physics that define the physical elements only cannot be the ultimate law. The Vedic law of cause and effect or elementary similarity defines the attraction between the entire spiritual, living, and non-living world. Everything is attracted towards its source. The fire on the earth is the part of the sun, the fire in the cosmos, as such the fire on earth is always attracted upwards towards its source.

Implied or suggested meaning: The intended meaning of the speaker may also suggest/imply or symbolise some particular or special sense other than the apparent one. For instance, if the speaker says: Taxi come here. Here, this sentence does not reflect the apparent meaning. The speaker does not want to call a taxi or to make the taxi hear him. But here this sentence suggests that the taxi driver should bring a taxi. Similarly if one calls a 'miser man' a 'great donor', that never means that the 'miser man' is a 'great donor', but the same is the satire that suggests the misery of the miser. The implied or suggested meaning may be known through context. As such to know the actual intention of the speaker the whole context is to be known. Statements often quoted out of contexts do not convey the actual intended sense of the speakers. Similarly, various rituals described in various texts also suggest some different meaning than what is actually performed.

Words are also of three types: vernacular, literary, and Vedic. Vernacular words are used by common men in society. They know their words, meaning, and intention. For instance, if somebody says about the marriage of his/her daughter that the family of the bridegroom is 'khāti piti hai' that means that the family is 'well to do'. On the other hand, if somebody says that I am not ready to marry my daughter in that particular family because that family is 'khāne pine wāli hai' that means that the family members are non-vegetarian and drunkards. The same words 'khānā-pīnā' have been used in two different meanings. Thus in vernacular languages, words, and their intended meaning are popularly known to the common men in the society.

On the other hand, common men are not able to understand the words, meanings, and intended sense of the literary language. For that, the help of a teacher is required. For instance, there is śloka:

केशवं पतितं दृष्टवा द्रोणो हर्षमुपागतः ।

रुदन्ति कौरवाः सर्वे हा हा केशव केशव।।

keśavaṁ patitaṁ dṛṣṭavā droṇo harṣam upāgataḥ
rudanti kauravāḥ sarve hā hā keśava keśava.

The apparent meaning of this śloka is

(*dṛṣṭavā*) Having seen (*keśavaṁ*) Kṛṣṇa (*patitaṁ*) falling on the ground, (*droṇo*) Droṇācharya (*harṣam upāgataḥ*) became very happy, (*kauravāḥ sarve*) but the Kaurava camp (*rudanti hā hā keśava keśava*) was in grief at the death of Kṛṣṇa.

Here this meaning becomes a great puzzle for the listener when Krishna was not fighting in the war, how can he fall down in the battlefield? How can Droṇa be happy and Kauravas be grieved at the fall of Krishna? At such places, the teachers can be the guiding force. The teachers interpret the above śloka as under:

(*dṛṣṭvā*) Having seen (*śava*) dead body (*patitaṁ*) lying (*ke*) in waters. (*droṇo*) birds (*harṣam upāgataḥ*) became happy, but all (*kauravas*) jackals were crying oh (*ke śava*) the dead body is in the waters, (*ke śava*) dead body is in the waters.

This shows that birds were having uninterrupted access to a dead body in the waters, but jackals were not having access to the same in waters, so they were crying being deprived of their food.

These were some illustrations about vernacular and literary words. Now we can take up some Vedic puzzles. Teachers cannot be the guiding force behind the solution of Vedic puzzles, but the seers can throw light on them. For example, we can take up a Mantra from the *Yajurveda* (23.20). The Mantra goes like this:

त उभौ चतुरः पदः संप्रसारयावः ।

tā ubhau caturaḥ padaḥ saṁprasārayāvaḥ

Which literally means that both of them should spread their four legs properly. Now the question arises as to who are they both? How come both of them have four legs? This is beyond the comprehension of both learned and laity. Because a man has two legs, how can he spread four legs?

If two persons unitedly spread four legs, the question arises what is the purpose behind this? Because spreading legs is not the cultured way of sitting. As such this Mantra of the Veda remained a puzzle unsolved for centuries. When we were not able to solve the puzzle, we approached the teachers/Āchāryas. Our Āchāryas Uvaṭa and Mahidhara inform us that this Mantra is obscene. This Mantra tells about a special type of sleeping style of the queen with the horse of Aśvamedha Yajña. This explanation raised two more questions. Do the Vedas contain obscene descriptions? The meeting of man and woman for procreating progeny is natural, but the meeting of a human female with an animal. seems like a talk of a fool of the first water. The doubt is that horse has four legs while a lady has two, so both together make six. Thus either the interpretation of Āchāryas is far fetched one or the Mantra does not have this intended sense.

When Āchāryas were not able to solve this puzzle, we approached seers. The earlier seers are not before us, so we saluted them as- नमः ऋषिभ्यः पूर्वजेभ्यः *namaḥ ṛṣibhyaḥ pūrvajebhyaḥ*. But in present times we have one seer with us. He is Maharishi Dayanand Sarasvati. When we referred to his Vedabhāṣya, all of our doubts are over. We had a doubt about the two things mentioned in the Veda, the seer says they are king and his subjects. How can a king and his subjects spread four legs? These four legs are four puruṣ ārthas-dharma, artha, kāma and mokṣa. Here the meaning is that both king and his subjects spread the four puruṣ ārthas.

Thus Ṛṣi Dayananda's Vedabhāṣya gives us to understand the factual clue of the Vedic Mantras. This Mantra like others has a simile, where the term expressing a simile is absent. Thus figuratively, this Mantra also points out the teacher and preacher who are a catalyst for the proliferation of puruṣārthas in the society.

Interpretations of the Vedas

The Vedas are the foremost record of the great advance made by humanity. They are the oldest literary compositions now available not only in the library of India but also in the library of the world.

They were visualised by the high-profile ṛṣis in their samādhi, or in course of doing the science of Mantra.[19] Those ṛṣis who visualised the Mantras or the Vedas were known as Sākṣākṛtadharmā Ṛṣis. Yāska, an ancient Indian Vedic Scholar makes a pointed reference to this fact as:

साक्षात्कृतधर्माणः ऋषयो बभूवुः ।

sākṣāt kṛta-dharmāṇaḥ ṛṣayo babhūvuḥ[20]

'There were born ṛṣis who visualised the Vedas.'

This knowledge was further passed on by oral instructions to the subsequent *ṛṣis* who couldn't visualise it. Thus arrangements were made to preserve this knowledge by way of a long uninterrupted reliable tradition of the successive ṛṣis. By and by, the number of visualised Mantras increased immensely and consequently a great bulk of subsidiary pronouncement thereof also came into being. This made the subsequent inheritors overburdened with Mantras and subsidiary pronouncements thereof. As such it became quite impossible for them to carry this big load of oral material by heart and thereby imparting it to next inheritors through oral instructions. Having tired of carrying this big load by heart, they subjected it to compilation and documentation for the referential work of future generations.

Yāska records this fact as:

ते अवरेभ्योऽसाक्षत्कृतधर्मभ्य उपदेशेन मन्त्रान्सम्प्रादुः । उपदेशाय

19. There are three types of science, Māntrika, Yāntrika and Tāntrika. For more details see the author (1993 : 84-101).

20. *Nir.* 1.20.

ग्लायन्तोऽवरे बिल्मग्रहणायेमं समाम्नासिषुर् वेदं च वेदान् च वेदांगानि च बिल्मं भिल्मं भासनमिति वा।

te avarebhyo'sākṣātkṛtadharmabhya upadeśena mantrān samprāduḥ. upadeśāya glāyanto' vare bilmagrahaṇāyemaṁsamāmnāsıṣur vedaṁ ca vedāṅ ca vedāṅgāni ca bilmaṁ bhilmaṁ bhāsanamiti vā.[21]

'They passed this knowledge on to the subsequent ṛṣis who couldn't visualise it by way of oral instructions. The subsequent inheritors having tired of imparting oral instructions to their successors, compiled/documented the Vedas and their subsidiary sciences or help books so as to make it intelligible to the future generations.'

Thus the Vedic tradition registered a transition in its history when the oral material was subjected to documentation. In fact, it was a transition from the auditory phase to the documentary phase. After the documentation of the Vedas and their subsidiary sciences, the Śruti paramparā (auditory tradition) of preserving the Vedas switched over to the Āmnāya[22], in addition to the Śruti.

This change of phase in the history of Vedic tradition occurred long ago prior to the period of Yāska.

From the very beginning of their composition, the Vedas along with their intents were handed down by the original seers to their heirs. They continued to be preserved in the long uninterrupted tradition of Vedic scholiasts. De grado en grado with the passage of time, not only did the Mantras undergo several textual variations and alterations, but the actual intent also faded away from the memories of their inheritors. In view of these problems, the texts which were preserved orally were documented along with their intent in order to save them from further corruption and

---

21. *Ibid.*
22. See *Nir.* 1.1.1 *samāmnāyaḥ samāmnātaḥ*
Also *VD.* 1.1.3. *tadvacanād āmnāyasya prāmāṇyam*

deterioration. This fact has very aptly been alluded to by Yāska as:

उपदेशाय ग्लायन्तोऽवरे बिल्मग्रहणायेमम्
ग्रन्थं समाम्नासिषुर् वेदं च वेदान् च वेदांगानि च ।

upadeśāya glāyanto'vare bilmagrahaṇāyedaṁ
granthaṁ smāmnāsıṣurvedaṁ ca vedāṅgāni ca (*Nir.* 1.20)

Thus, it is clear from the foregoing that the Saṁhitās were compiled to preserve the Mantras and the subsidiary aids like the Vedāṅgas and the Brāhmaṇas were prepared to preserve their intent. It is thus proved that the process of interpretations of the Vedas is as old as their physical structure is.

Later on, when the subsidiary aids prepared for their elucidation and elaboration couldn't serve their purpose perfectly, attempts were made by ancient and medieval scholars to write separate commentaries on each and every extant Saṁhitā and its Brāhmaṇa so as to make their intents more intelligible to the subsequent scholars and students.

Padapāṭha School of the Vedic Interpretation

Various schools of Vedic interpretation owe their origin to the various methods applied by the actual seers and their successors for the onward transmission of the visualised Mantras to the successive inheritors from time to time.

The original seers of the Vedas taught their respective Mantras to the successive disciples by analysing the words into their component elements. This gave rise to the Padapāṭha school of Vedic interpretation which aimed at analysing the words into their components. It may also be said that Padapāṭha is the most ancient attempt of Vedic interpretation.

Here it may be pointed out that various pāṭhas popularly known as vikṛtis[23] such as Kramapāṭha, Jaṭāpāṭha, Mālāpāṭha, Śikhāpāṭha, Rekhāpaṭha, etc. which were invented by later ṛṣis to guard the Vedic texts from the possibility of any change or interpolations are all based on the Padapāṭha.

The various schools developed their distinct methods of Padapāṭha. Now we shall take stock of extant Padapāṭhas of various Saṁhitās that are available to us.

Śākalya (Dvāpara 863900, i.e. 100 years before Kaliyuga, i.e. 32 century BC) composed the Padapāṭha of the *Ṛgveda.*[24] Yāska (Kali 400, i.e. c. 28 century BC) and Patañjali (Kali 1000, i.e. c. 22 century BC) have questioned Śākalya's Padapāṭha at several places. For

---

23. *jaṭā māla śikhā rekhā dhvajo daṇḍo ratho ghanaḥ*
aṭau vikṛtayaḥ proktāḥ kramapūrvā mahaṛṣibhiḥ

24. *devamitraśca śākalyo mahātmā dvijapuṅgavaḥ*
cakāra saṁhitā pañca buddhimān padavittamaḥ
(*VP.* 60.63)

instance, Yāska challenges Śākalya's analysis of *vāya* [25] (*RV.* 10.29.1) as *vā* + *yaḥ* and *maāsakṛt* [26] (*RV.* 1.105.8.) as *māsa* + *kṛt.* However, Śaunaka, the author of *Bṛhaddevatā* favours Śākalya and sets aside Yāska's analysis without assigning any reason[27].

Patañjali in his *Mahābhāṣya* on Pāṇini's *sūtras*

एतिस्तुश्वृदृजुषः क्यप् ।

etistuśvṛdṛjuṣaḥ kyap [28]

अनो नुट् ।

ano nuṭ [29]

असितः कर्ता ।

āśitaḥ kartā. [30]

rejects Śākalya's analysis of *ājyam* [31], *āśitam* [32] and

---

25. *vane iva vāyaḥ ve putraḥ cāyan iti vā kāmayamānaḥ iti vā. vā iti ca yaḥ iti ca cakāra śākalyaḥ* (*Nir.* 6.28)

26. *māsakṛt māsāṁ cārdhamāsānāṁ ca karta. candramāḥ vṛkaḥ.* (*Nir.* 2.21)

27 *anekaṁ satthathā cānyad ekameva niruktavān aruṇo māsakṛnmantre māsakṛdvigraheṇa tu.*(BD. 2.112).

28 . 3.1.109.

29 . 8.2.16.

30 . 6.1.207.

31. It has occured in the *RV.* 10.90.6; 10.122.7; 10.130.3; 10.53.2; 10.88.4; 10.79.5 without *avagraha.* Patañjali suggests that it should be placed in Pāda text with *avagraha, ā'yam. āṅ pūrvasyaıṣa prayogo bhavıṣyati. yadyevamavagraḥprāpnoti. Mahabhāṣya* Part 3, P. 207 on Pāṇ. 3.1.109.

32. It is also used in the *RV.* 10.37.11; 10.117.1; 10.117.7 without *avagraha.* Here, too, Patañjali suggests *avagraha.* According to him: *añpūvasyaprayogaḥ.*

akṣaṛvān [33] and refers his own analysis in this regard. He asserts that grammarians should not follow Padakāras but Padakāras may, if necessary, follow grammar and the Padapāṭhas, or word analysis should be done in accordance with the rules of grammar.[34]

The Padapāṭha of the *Vājasaneyi Saṁhita* of *Yajurveda* (*VS*). and the *Atharvaveda* (*AV.*) are also available, but their composers' name is not known. Bhagavadatta assigns the authorship of the *Vājasaneyī Saṁhitā's* Padapāṭha to Kātyāyana (Kali 240, i.e. c. 2800 BC), but we do not come across any strong proof in support of his claim.

Ātareya (Kali 40 or c. 3000 BC) is the author of the Padapāṭha of the *Taittirīya Saṁhitā* (*TS*).[35] Gārgya

---

yadyevamavagraḥprāpnoti. Mahābhāṣya Part. 4, P. 530 on Pāñ. 6.1.207.

33. It occurs in *RV.* 1.164.16. Padakāra places it with *avagraha* as *akṣaṇ'vān.* Patañjali, however, suggests that it should be placed without avagraha. *avagrahaścāmṇe deśe prāpnoti - akṣaṇvāniti.*

(*Mahābhāṣya,* Part 5, P. 380, Pāṇ. 8.2.16).

asiddho nuṭ tasyā'siddhatvādbhaviṣyati - avagrahe'pi (*Mahābhāṣya,* Part 5, P. 382, Pāṇ. 8.2.16).

Cf. *Padamañjarī* on *Kāśikā* 8.2.16.

nanvevamapyavagrahe doṣaḥ prāpnoti akṣaṇvanta iti akṣaṇvante iti nāntamavagṛhṇāti tanna prāpnoti (*KV.* Part. IV, P. 374).

34. *na lakṣanena padakārā anuvartyāpadakārairnāma lakṣaṇamanu vartyam. yathālakṣaṇaṁ padaṁ karttvyam.* (*Mahābhāṣya,* on Pāṇ. 30.1.109.; 6.1.207.; 8.2.16)

35 Bhaṭabhāskara writes in his colophone to the *TS.* Bhāṣya *ukhaścātreyāya dadau yena padavibhāgaścakre*

A quotation from Bhagavadatta's *Vaidika Vāṅmaya kā itihāsa,* P. 157.

(Dvāpara 863900, i.e. c.3100BC) is credited with the Padapāṭha of the *Sāmaveda Saṁhitā* (*SV*). He analyses the padas into several constituents, e.g.

mitram into *mi + tram*

adya into *a + dya*

sakhye into *sa + khye*

śraddhā into *śrat + dhā*

candramasaḥ into *candra + masaḥ* [36]

Dūrga (Kali 2300, i.e. c. 800 BC) and Skandhaswamī (Kali 3800, i.e. c. 1300) point out to the same eccentric feature of Gārya's Padapāṭha in their respective commentaries on the *Nirukta*:

यन्म इह नास्ति वा त्रिणि मध्यमानि पदानि।

yanma iha nāstti vā trīṇi madhyamāni padāni [37] in the context of *mehana.*[38]

Yāska, however, accepts the authenticity of this Padapāṭha mostly banks on it for his etymologies, since he provides several of his etymologies in accordance with this Padapāṭha as it is obvious from the following comparison:

Gārgya's Padapāṭha	**Etymologies of Yāska**
mi + tram	*pramitestrāyate*[39]

---

36 . See for detail, Bhgavadatta P. 159.

37 . *Nir.* 4. 4.

38. See Skandhabhāṣya on *Nir.* 4.4. as follows :

ekamiti śākalyaḥ trīṇiti gārgyaḥ--------chandogānāntu mehanā śabdo naivāsit yadindra citra ma iha nāsti - ityevarāpaḥ pāṭhaḥ teṣāṁ - citra/me/iha/nāsti. ityeṣāṁ padānāṁ me/iha/na/ityevaṁ rūpāṇi madhyamāni padāni.

Also see Durgavṛtti on *Nir.* 4.4.

a + dya	*asmin dyavi*[40]
sa + khye	*samāna khyānā*[41]
śrat + dhā	*śraddhānāt*[42]
candra + masaḥ	*candro māta*[43]
sama + udram	*samuddravantyasmādāpaḥ*[44]
duḥ + āt	*durayaṁ vā*[45]
su + astaye	*su astīti*[46]
u + striyāḥ	*usrāviṇo's syāṇbhogāḥ*[47]
put + trasya	*punnarakaṁ tatastrāyata iti*[48]

Padapāṭha of the *Atharvaveda* (*AV.*) is similar to that of the *Ṛgveda* (*RV.*)

There are basic differences in the technique of word analysis of various Padakāras. For instance:

Padakāras of the *RV.* and the *AV.* don't repeat the words after avagraha, as for example:

paraḥ ' hitam[49]

tri ' saptāḥ[50]

On the other hand, Padakāras of the *VS. TS.*, *MS.* and *SV.* apply *iti* and repeat the *pada* to show *avagraha*, e.g.

श्रेष्ठतमायेति श्रेष्ठऽतमाय

---

39 . *Nir.* 10.21.
40 . *Ibid.* 1.6.
41 . *Ibid.* 7.30.
42 . *Ibid.* 9.30.
43 . *Ibid.* 11.5.
44 . *Ibid.* 2.10.
45 . *Ibid.* 3.19.
46 . *Ibid.* 3.21.
47 . *Ibid.* 4.19.
48 . *Ibid.* 2.1.
49 . *RV.* 1.1.1.
50 . *AV.* 1.1.1.

śreṭhatamāyeti śreṭha'tamāya.[51]

श्रेष्ठतमायेति श्रेष्ठऽतमाय

śreṭhatamāyeti śreṭha'tamāya.[52]

Iva is treated as a part of the preceding word by the Padakāras of the *RV.*, *VS.*, *AV.* and *MS.* e.g.

पितैऽइव *pitāi 'iva*[53]

पितैऽइव *pitāi 'iva*[54]

राजेवेति राजाऽइव *rājeveti rājā 'iva*[55]

वस्नेवेति वस्नाऽइव *vasneveti vasnā'iva*[56]

on the other hand, *iva* is treated as an independent word by the Padakāras of the *SV.* and *TS.* e.g.

क्षोणिः +इव *kṣoṇiḥ + iva*[57]

राजा +इव *rājā + iva*[58]

(3). Iti is added after the pragṛhya vowels by the Padakāras of the *RV.*, *SV.*, *AV.*, *TS.* and *MS.* e.g.

वाये इति *vāyo iti*[59]

त्वे इति *tve iti*[60].

अस्मे इति *asme iti*[61]

विष्णो इति *visṇo iti*[62]

However, the Padakāra of the *VS.* repeats the pada

---

51 . *VS.* 1.1.
52 . *TS.* 1.1.1.; *MS.* 1.1.1.
53 . *RV.* 1.1.1.
54 . *AV.* 2.13.1.
55 . *VS.* 13.9.
56 . *MS.* 1.10.2.
57 . *SV.* 4.4.4.
58 . *TS.* 1.2.14.; 28.
59 . *RV.* 1.2.3.; *AV.* 6.68.1.
60 . *SV.* 1.1.3.
61 . *SV.* 2.1.3.
62 . *TS.* 1.1.3.; *MS.* 1.1.3.

after 'iti'. [63]

Skandha also observes this difference in the technique of various Padakāras in his commentary on the *Nir.* 2.13. in the context of the etymology of *ādityaḥ* as under:

śāklyātreya prabhṛtibhir nāvagṛhītam. Pūrvanirvacanābhiprāye gārgya prabhṛtibhir avagṛrhītam. vicitrāḥ padakārāṇāmabhiprāyāḥ. kvacidupasarga vıṣaye'pi nāvagṛhṇanti yathā śākalyena 'adhivāsam' iti nāvagṛhītam. tasmā 'navagraha iti.'

'Śākalya and others didn't apply *avagraha.* In the context of the first etymology. Gārgya and others applied *avagraha.* Padakāras have different opinions. Some times they don't apply avagraha in the context of prepositions, as for example, Sākalya doesn't apply *avagraha in the analysis of adhi + vāsam'.*

Yudhiṣthira Mimāṁsaka (1909-1994) details many other differences of Padapāṭhas in his introduction.[64]

The utility of Padapāṭha in the interpretation of the Vedas

Padapāṭha is the first requirement for the interpretation of the Vedas. Padapāṭha analyses the Saṁhitā-text into Pāda-text, thus providing the groundwork for the interpretation of the Vedas. All other schools of Vedic interpretation do rely upon the Padapāṭhas for their interpretation of the Saṁhitās always depends upon the correct analysis of the padas, correct knowledge of the position of accent on individual words and correct impounding the compounds. This is only possible through Padapāṭha. A correct Padapāṭha helps in correct etymology and thereby correct interpretation of the Vedas.

The advantage of Pāda-text in a better understanding of the Vedic texts has been accepted by Yāska in the following

---

63. *VS.* 1.4.

64. *Cf. PP.* 11-26

text of the *Niruka.* [65]

अवसाय पदवते रुद्र मृळ इति *avasāya padavate rudra mṛl iti* (*RV.* 10.169.1)

अवतेर्गत्यर्थस्यासौ नामकरण *avatergatyarthasyāsau nāmakaraṇaḥ*

तस्मान्नावगृहणन्ति अवसायाश्वान् इति *tasmānnāvagṛhaṇanti avasāyāśvān iti* (*RV.* 1.104.1)

स्यतिरुपसृ विमोचने तस्मादवगृहणन्ति पदकारः *syatirupasṛ vimocane tasmād avagṛhaṇanti Padakārāḥ*

In the Ṛgvedic verse *'avasāya padvate', 'avasāya'* is a nominal formation, so Padakāra doesn't apply *avagraha* in its analysis. On the other hand in the Ṛgvedic verse *'avasāyāśvān'* it is a verbal formation formed from the verb '*syati'* preceded by preposition '*ava'*, meaning 'to free'. Therefore, the Padakāra, apply *avagraha* in its analysis.'

---

65. 1.17.

Yājñika School of the Vedic Interpretation

The Vedas are the oldest book available in the library of the world. From the very beginning the *vedārtha* was preserved by a tradition of Vedic seers, but with the passage of time this long, uninterrupted reliable tradition, began to fizzle out. Consequently, the original significance of the Vedic Mantras became difficult and so was forgotten. Later on, many schools came forward for the preservation of the Vedas and the *vedārtha.* All of them with their distinct styles and methods tried to revive the lost significance of the Vedas. Prominent among those were Padapāṭhakāras, Yājñikas, Aitihāsikas, Nairuktas and Naidānas, etc. All of the schools attempted to give an easy and approachable pathway to the original vedārtha by way of their unique styles and methods based on the vedārtha handed down to them traditionally by their predecessors. Although it's a fact that Padapāṭha was the first attempt to safeguard the Veda from destruction and interpolations and provided a foundation to other schools of Vedic interpretation, but the first systematic effort to preserve vedārtha was made by Yājñikas, who in the Brāhmaṇas revealed the esoteric significance of the difficult words attested in the Vedic verses.

The Yajñikas taught the intended significance of various *padas* occurring in the Vedic stanza. For instance, while teaching the intended significance of 'agni', 'palāsa' or 'aśva', etc., the seer taught his heir as under:

अग्निर्वै ब्रह्म *agnir vai brahma*, 'Agni' signifies here 'brahma'.

पलाशो वै ब्रह्म *palāśo vai brahma*, 'palāśa' signifies here 'brahma'.

क्षत्रं वा अश्वः '*kṣratraṁ vā aśvaḥ*', 'aśva' signifies here 'kṣatrīya'.

यज्ञो वै विष्णुः *yajño vai viṣṇu,* 'Yajña' signifies here 'Viṣ ṇu'.

प्राणो वा अंगिरा *prāṇo vā aṅgirāḥ,* 'aṅgirā' signifies here 'prāṇa'.

In the above-cited examples, the use of particles like 'vai' or 'vā' indicates that the word under reference was made known by the actual seer in a particular meaning to his heir, Sāyaṇa (Kali 4418-4490, i.e. c. 1428-1500) also narrates this fact as:

वै शब्दः उक्तार्थे मन्त्र प्रसिद्धि द्योतनार्थः ।

vai śabdaḥ uktārthe Mantra prasiddhi dyotanārthaḥ. [66]

'The particle 'vai' indicates the popularity of the Mantra in the said meaning.'

The traditional heirs of the Vedas also while teaching the inherited Mantras to the subsequent inheritors quoted meanings known to them by way of the tradition inherited by them. Apart from quoting for their successors the hereditary meanings, they also quoted sometimes such meanings as were made known in the family or school of some other seers. While quoting such meanings as borrowed from other family or school, the heirs used the particle 'hi', as for example *jyotir hi hiraṇyam,* i.e. 'in the family or school of some other seer, 'jyoti' signifies 'hiraṇya'.

Sāyaṇa could acknowledge this fact through the tradition inherited by him. He had it as:

श्रुत्यन्तर प्रसिद्धि द्योतनार्थः हि शब्दः

śrutyantra prasiddhi dyotanārthaḥ hi śabdaḥ [67]

'The particle 'hi' is used to indicate the meaning popular in the tradition of some other school.'

Thus it is clear from the aforementioned discussion that

66 . See Sāyaṇa Bhāṣya on the the *A.Br.* 1.1.1.

67 . *ibid.*

the visualised Mantras were passed on by the actual seers to their heirs along with their intent. The intended sense along with the *Mantras* also continued to flow in the long uninterrupted tradition of the subsequent heirs of the actual seers. When the long uninterrupted Vedic tradition registered a change of phase in its history, i.e. instead of preserving the bulky Vedic literature in auditory form, it was subjected to documentation or say began to be preserved in a documentary form, the inherited intent of the Vedas was documented in the name of the Brāhmaṇas. Each family or school of the Vedic seers documented its own Brāhmaṇa. This is why we find each and every school of the Veda represented by its own Brāhmaṇa text.

In fact, the word 'Brāhmaṇa' is etymolised as ब्रह्म जानाति ब्राह्मणम् *Brahma jānātīti Brāhmaṇam.*

'Brāhmaṇa' is the text that explains 'Brahman'.

'Brahma' here is the intent of the pada contained in the Mantra. The concept of Śabda-brahma also substantiates the fact that padārtha (meaning) of pada (word) is 'Brahma' and the act of studying Vedas is called as Brahmacarya Vrata and whoever observed this vrata or wanted to study the Vedas was called as Brahmcārī. However, the terms Brahmacarya and Brahmacārī now are used in altogether a changed meaning. So, Mantra and brahma were two different terms. Mantras were visualised by the seers and Brahma (meaning) of Mantras was made known by them to their heirs. By way of documentation, Mantras were compiled separately as *Saṁhitās* and brahma (meaning) was explained in the *Brāhmaṇas.* Since Brāhmaṇa text was taught or handed over simultaneously by the actual seer to his heir, the dictum -

मन्त्र ब्राह्मणोर्वेदनामधेयम् ।

Mantra-brāhmaṇayor veda nāmadheyam [68]

i.e. both Mantra and its brāmaṇa should be known

---

68 . *Āpastamba Yajña Paribhāṣā*, 1.1.31.

by the name Veda - also came into vogue.

There ensued heated debates and discussions among scholars on the issue as to whether the Mantra alone or the Mantra along with its brāhmaṇa should be known by the name of Veda. Records of this type of debates and discussions only mark the phases of darkness that prevailed over in the history of Vedic exegesis. At this stage, it is not important to discuss whether the Mantra alone or along with its brāhmaṇa should be known as Veda, but it is most important and imperative on the part of a serious Vedic researcher to know that the traditionally inherited actual intent of the Mantras handed down to the heirs and later preserved in the extant *Brāhmaṇas* is in its intact form and could not be obliterated with the ravages of time. Yāska's following observations shed an ample good light on the nature and style of the *Brāhmaṇa Granthas.* He observes,

बहु भक्ति वादिनि हि ब्राह्मणानि भवन्ति। पृथिवी वैश्वानरः। संवत्सरो वैश्वानरः। ब्राह्मणो वैश्वानर इति।

bahu bhakti vādini hi brāhmaṇni bhavanti.
pṛthivi vaiśvānaraḥ saṁvatsaro vaiśvānara, brāhmaṇo vaiśvānara iti. [69]

'The *Brāhmaṇas* speak of various parallel meanings based upon various characteristics of one and the same deity, such as the earth is 'vaiśvānara'; the year is 'vaiśvānara'; the brahmaṇa is 'vaiśvānara', etc.'

So far as the question of authenticity of the meaning preserved in the *Brāhmaṇas* is concerned, the authenticity of various meanings envisaged in the *Brāhmaṇas* may be confirmed only in the light of the Vedas. Here it may be pointed out that the various meanings revealed in the *Brāhmaṇas* derive their support from the various passages of the Vedas. The studies of the present author have proved that the various words used in the passages of the Vedas as

---

69 . *Nir.* 7.24

attributive epithets or predictive of some words have also appeared in the *Brāhmaṇas* as the synonym of the same word that was qualified by them in the Vedas.

The following examples suffice to prove the above statement.

1. In the Veda, 'pṛthivī' or 'bhūmi' is called 'mātā', e.g.

माता भूमि पुत्रोऽहं पृथिव्याः ।

'mātā bhūhmi putro haṁ pṛthivyāḥ.' [70]

पृथिवी माता

'pṛthivī mātā' [71]

उपहूता पृथिवी मातोपमां पृथिवी माता ह्वयताम् ।

'upahūtā pṛthivī-mātopamāṁ pṛthivī mātā hvayatām' [72]

इयं पृथिवी वै माता

'iyam (pṛthivi) vai mātā' [73]

The Brāhmaṇas also explain 'pṛthvī' as 'mātā'.

पृथिवीं मातरं महीम्

'pṛthivīṁ mātaraṁ mahīm' [74]

'Pṛthivī' is addressed as 'mahī' in the Veda, e.g.

भूमिं महीम् अपाराम् । '*bhūmiṁ mahīm apārām*' [75]

यथेयं पृथिवी मही दाधार । '*yatheyam pṛthivī mahī dādhāra*' [76]

पृथिवीं मातरं महीम अन्तरिक्षम् उपब्रुवे । '*pṛthivīṁ mātaraṁ mahīm antarikṣam uparuve*' [77]

---

70 . *AV.* 12.12.
71 . *MS.* 4.2.10.
72 . *VS.* 2.1.
73 . *Ś.Br.* 13.1.6.1.
74 . *MS.* 3.2.9.; *TS.* 3.8.9.; *T.Br.* 2.4.68.
75 . *RV.* 3.30.9.
76 . *ibid.* 10.6.9.
77 . *TS.* 4.6.8.

Similarly, the Brāhmaṇas define 'pṛthivī' as 'mahī'.

इयं पृथिवीं वै माहीनम *'iyaṁ (pṛthivī) vai māhīnam'* [78]

इयं पृथिवी एव मही। *'iyaṁ (pṛthivī) eva māhī'* [79]

इयं पृथिवी महती। *'iyaṁ (pṛthivī) mahatī'* [80]

पृथिवी मातरं महीम्। *'pṛthivīṁ mātaraṁ mahīm'* [81]

3. In the Veda 'pṛthivī' has frequently been attributed to 'urvī' as :

उर्वी पृथ्वी *'urvī pṛthvī'* [82]

उर्वी पृथिवी *'urvī pṛthivī'* [83]

उर्वीं पृथिवीं *'urvīṁ pṛthivīṁ'* [84]

पृथिवीभूतमुर्वी *'pṛthivī bhūtamurvī'* [85]

The Brāhmaṇas also recall pṛthivī as urvī, e.g.

यथेयं पृथिव्युर्वी एवमुरुभूयासम् *'yatheyaṁ pṛthiviyurvī evamurubhūyāsam'* [86]

The Veda proclaims 'aśva' as 'āśu', as in

आशुमश्वम् *'āśum aśvam'* [87]

The Brāhmaṇas also explain 'aśva' as 'āśu', e.g.

आशु सप्तिरित्याहा। अश्व एव जवं दधाति। तस्मात् पुराशुरश्वोऽजायत्।

'āśu saptirityāha. aśva eva javaṁ dadhāti. tasmāt purāśurśvo jāyata' [88]

78 . *A.Br.* 3.38.
79 . *Ju. Br.* 3.1.4.2; 7.
80 . *Ś.Br.* 1.5.
81 . *T.Br. 2.4.6.8.*
82 . *RV.* 1.185.7.
83 . *ibid.* 6.1.7.
84 . *ibid.* 7.38.2.
85 . *ibid.* 6.68.4.
86 . *Ś.Br.* 2.1.4.28.
87 . *RV.* 7.71.5.
88 . *T.Br.* 3.4.13.2

आश्वः पशूनामाशुः सारसारियामहः ।

'āśvaḥ paśūnāmāśuḥ sārasāriamaḥ' [89]

5. The Veda exhibits the comparison of 'aśva' with 'vājī' as evident from the following:

अश्वं न वाजिनम् ।

'aśvaṁ na vājinam' [90]

अश्वं न त्वा वाजिनम् ।

'aśvaṁ na tvā vājinam' [91]

Likewise, 'aśva' has been regarded as 'vājī' in the Brāhmaṇas as:

वाजिन ह्यश्वाः ।

vājin hyaśvāḥ' [92]

वाजी (भूत्वाऽवः) गन्धर्वानवहत् ।

'vājī (bhūtva' śvaḥ) gandharvān (avahat)' [93]

6. One more interesting example invites out attention. In the Veda, 'aśva' has been compared with 'vājī', e.g.

अश्वं न वाजिनम् ।

'aśvam na vājinam' [94]

'atya' with 'vājī' as in

अत्यं न वाजिनम् ।

'atyaṁ na vājinam' [95]

अत्यो न वाजी ।

'atyo na vājī' [96]

---

89 . *ibid.* 3.8.7.1.
90 . *RV.* 7.7.1.
91 . *ibid.* 9.8.7.1.
92 . *Kāṭh. S.* 5.28.4.; *Kaṭh. S.* 4.4.4.; *Ś.Br.* 2.1.4.15
93 . *Ś.Br.* 10.6.4.1.
94 . *RV.* 7.7.1.
95 . *ibid.* 1.135.5.

and atya with sapti as

अत्यं न सप्तिम्।

'atyaṁ na saptim' [97]

On the contrary, the *Tāṇḍ. Br.* quotes all these 'aśva', 'vājī' and 'sapti' as the alternative terms, e.g.

अश्वोस्यत्योऽसि मयोसि हयोसि वाज्यसि सप्तिरस्युर्वासि वृषासि।

'aśvo syatyosi mayosi hayosi vājyasi saptirasyurvāsi vṛṣāsi' [98]

7. 'Sarasvatī', in the Veda, has been supplied with such attributive epithet as 'vāk', e.g.

यं याचाम्यहं वाचा सरस्वत्या *'yaṁ yācāmyahaṁ vācā sarasvatyā'* [99]

When we come down to the Brāhmaṇās we find the same 'sarastvatī' as an attrbutive of 'vāk', e.g.

वाचं सरस्वतीं स्वाहाकारेण परिगृह्णीयात् *'vācaṁ sarasvatīṁ svāhākāreṇa parigṛhṇiyāt'* [100]

वाचे सरस्वत्यै स्वाहा *'vāce sarasvatyai svāhā'* [101]

But sometimes we see that 'vāk' has been given the designation of 'sarasvatī'. e.g.

वागेव सरस्वती *'vāgeva saraswatī'* [102]

8. In the Veda, we chance upon 'saha' as the adjective of 'oja', e.g. *'saha vai ojaḥ'* [23]

The Brāhmaṇas have taken 'saha' and 'oja' as the alternative words for each other. e.g.

---

96. *ibid.* 9.96.15.
97. *ibid.* 3.22.1.
98. *Tāṇḍ Br.* 1.7.1.
99. *RV.* 1.7.1.
100. *J.Br.* 1.82.
101. *T.Ār*, 4.5.1.
102. *A.Br.* 2.24.; 6.7.
23. RV. *5.57.6.*

ओजो सहः सह ओजः *'ojaḥ sahaḥ saha ojaḥ'* [24]

9. 'Vāk', in the Veda, has been attributed to 'ṛk', as

ऋचं वाचं प्रपद्ये *'ṛcaṁ vācaṁ prapadye'* [25]

Further down in the Brāhmaṇas 'ṛk' has been depicted as one of the three divisions of 'vāk', e.g.

त्रेधा विहिता हि वाक्. ऋचो यजुंषि सामानि *'tredhā vihitā hi vāk ṛco yajuṁṣi sāmāni.* [26]

10. In the Veda, sun rays have been proclaimed as, 'acchidra pavitra' 'a sieve without holes'.

For instance,

अच्छिद्रेण पवित्रेण सूर्यस्य रश्मिभिः।*'acchidreṇa pavitreṇ sūryasya raśmibhiḥ'* [27]

Later in the Brāhmaṇa portion, the same has been exposed as 'acchidra pavitra', as in

एतदेवा अच्छिद्रेण पवित्रेण यत् सूर्यस्य रश्मयः।

'etadevā acchidreṇa pavitreṇa yat sūryasya raśmayaḥ' [28]

11. 'Pṛthivī' has been described as 'devayajanī' in the Veda, as

पृथिवी देवयजनि। *'pṛthivī devayajanī'* [29]

Later, the Brāhmaṇas also take it to mean as 'devayajanī' and they call 'devayajana' as the 'mūrdhā' (forehead) of 'pṛthivī', e.g.

इयं वै पृथिवी देवी देवयजनी *'iyaṁ vai pṛthivī devī devayajanī'* [30]

---

24. Kau. Br. *13.5*
25. VS. 3.61
26. Ś.Br. *6.5.3.4.; 10.4.5.2.*
27. VS. 1.12.; 1.131.; 4.4.
28. MSB. 3.6.3.; 4.4.2.
29. VS. *1.25; 3.5.*
30. *Ś.Br.* 3.2.2.20.

भौमं देवयजनम् *'bhaumaṁ devayajanam'*[31]

पृथिव्या ह्येष मूर्धा यद् देवयजनम्। *'pṛthivyā hyeṣa mūrdhā yad devayajanam'*[32]

एष ह वै पृथिव्या मूर्धा यद् देवयजनम्। *'eṣa ha vai pṛthivyā mūrdhā yad devayajanam'*[33]

12. In the Veda, 'dyāvā-pṛthivī' has been recognized with 'mitrā-varuṇau', as *'dyāvāpṛthivī-mitrāvaruṇau'*[34]

Further down we find that Brāhmaṇakāras have presented 'dyāvā-pṛthivī' as the lovely home of 'mitrā-varuṇa', e.g.

द्यावापृथिवी वै मित्रावरुणयोः प्रियं धाम।*'dyāvāpṛthivī vai mitrāvaruṇayoḥ priyaṁ dhāma'*[35]

13. The Veda quotes 'agni' as 'gṛhapati', e.g.

अग्ने गृहपते। *'agne gṛhapate'*[36]

अयमग्निर्गृहपतिः। 'ayamagnirgṛhapatiḥ'[37]

The Brāhmaṇas also reveal the popularity of 'agni' as 'gṛhapati', as in

अयमग्निर्गृहपतिरिति हैक आहुः। सोऽस्य लोकस्य गृहपतिः।

'agnirgṛhapatiriti haika āhūḥ. so'sya lokasya gṛhapatiḥ'[38]

अथयदग्निं गृहपतिमन्तो यजति। *'athayadagniṁ gṛhapatimantato yajati'*[39]

14. In the Veda, 'agni' is attributed to 'vratapati', as

अग्ने व्रतपते व्रतं चरिष्यामि। *'agne vratapate vrataṁ*

---

31. *G.Br.* 1.2.14.
32. *T.Br.* 6.1.8.2.
33. *MSB.* 3.7.6.; *Kāṭh.S.* 2.4.4.; *Kaṭh.S.* 37.5
34. *VS.* 2.16.
35. *Tāṇḍ. Br.* 14.2.4
36. *VS.* 2.27.
37. *ibid.* 3.39.
38. *A.Br.* 5.24.
39. *Kau. Br.* 3.9.

carisyāmi' [40]

The Brāhmannas also recognize 'agni' in the form of 'vratapati', e.g.

अग्निर्वै देवानां व्रतपतिः '*agnir vai devānām vratapatiḥ*' [41]

अग्निर्वै देवानां व्रतभृत् '*agnir vai devānām vratabhṛt*' [42]

Hosts of similar other examples may be cited which would give an outright support to the author's opinion that the explanatory notes or stanzas of the *Brāhmaṇas* are nothing else but the traditionally inherited meaning of the Veda. They are based on the Veda itself. Being in conformity with the Veda, they are quite authentic and acceptable. But to our surprise, some modern scholars due to lack of study and proper guidelines of research into Vedic studies consider the Brāhmaṇic explanatory formulae as mere farce and baseless suppositions.

The subject matter of the Brāhmaṇas

Here it is also pertinent to mention that the actual subject-matter of the Brāhmaṇas was handed over by the actual seers and early heirs to their respective successors.

The early Brāhmaṇas, as has been explained earlier, contained only the explanatory statements. They spoke only of various meanings identified by various seers in the beginning. It is clear from Yāska's statement already quoted above. I repeat the same hereunder:

बहु भक्ति वादिनि हि ब्राह्मणानि भवन्ति। पृथिवी वैश्वानरः। संवत्सरो वैश्वानरः। ब्राह्मणो वैश्वानर इति।

bahu bhakti vādini hi brāhmaṇni bhavanti.
pṛthivi vaiśvānaraḥ saṁvatsaro vaiśvānara, brāhmaṇo vaiśvānara iti. [69]

---

40. *VS.* 2.22.
41. *Ś.Br.* 1.1.1.2.; 3.2.2.22.; G.Br. 2.1.1.4.
42. *G.Br.* 2.1.1.5.
69. *Nir.* 7.24

'The Brāhmaṇas speak of various parallel meanings based upon various characteristics of one and the same deity, such as the earth is 'vaiśvānara'; the year is 'vaiśvānara'; the Brāhmaṇa is 'vaiśvānara', etc.'

Thus, it can unhesitatingly be said that the earlier Brāhmaṇas were known only for their explanatory statements.

Yāska has quoted the views of the Brāhmaṇas at many places while attempting the etymology of various Vedic vocables in his *Nirukta*. For instance,

1. पंचर्तवः संवत्सरस्य इति च ब्राह्मणम्।
   pañcartavaḥ saṁvatsarasya iti ca brāhmaṇam. [70]

   'There are five seasons in a year', says Brāhmaṇas.

2. षष्टिश्च ह वै त्रीणि च शतानि संवत्सरस्याहोरात्राः। इति च ब्राह्मणं समासेन।
   ṣaṣṭiśca vai trīṇ ca śatāni saṁvatsarasy-āhorātrāḥ iti brāhmaṇam samāsena. [71]

   'There are 360 days in a year', the Brāmaṇas had it briefly.

3. सप्त च वै शतानि विंशतिश्च संवत्सरस्याहोरात्राः इति च ब्राह्मणं विभागेन।
   sapta ca vai śatāni viṁśatiśca saṁvatsarasyāhorātrāḥ iti ca brāhmaṇaṁ vibhāgena. [72]

   'As per division made in the *Brāhmaṇas*, a year consists of 720 days and nights.'

4. वराहो मेघो भवति वराहारः 'वरमाहारमाहार्षीः' इति च ब्राह्मणम्।

   varāho megho bhavati varāhāraḥ 'varamāhāıṣīḥ' iti ca brāhmaṇam. [73]

---

70 . *Nir.* 4.27.
71 . *Nir.* 4.27
72 . *ibid.* 4.27
73. *ibid.* 5.21.

'Varāha' is the cloud since it brings good provisions. It is the harbinger of good provisions, according to the Brāhmaṇas.'

5. पूषेत्यपरं सोऽदन्तकः। 'अदन्तकः पूषा' इति च ब्राह्मणम्।

pūṣeṭyaparaṁ so adantakaḥ 'adantakaḥ pūṣā' iti ca brāhmaṇam. [74]

'Another meaning of 'Pūṣā' is 'adantaka', as the Brāhmaṇas had it 'puṣā adantaka', i.e. 'pūṣā' is 'adantaka'.'

6. गायत्री गायतेः स्तुतिकर्मणः। त्रिगमना वा विपरीता गायता मुखादुदपतदिति च ब्राह्मणम्।

gāyatrī gāyateḥ stutikarmaṇaḥ trigamanā vā, viparītā gāyato mukhādudapataditi ca brāhmaṇam. [75]

'Gāyatrī' is formed from the root √gi 'to sing in praise'. It consists of three pādas. According to the Brāhmaṇas, it was named Gāyatrī because it originated from the mouth of the singer.'

7. अनुष्टुबनुष्टोभनात्। गायत्रीमेव त्रिपदां सतीं चतुर्थेन पादेनानुष्टोभतीति च ब्राह्मणम्।

anuṣṭubanuṣṭobhanāt gāyatrīmeva tri padāṁ satīṁ aturthena pādenānuṭobhatī ti ca brāhmaṇam.[76]

'Anuṣṭubha' formed from the root √stu prefixed by 'anu'. According to the Brāhmaṇas, it was sung after 'Gāyātrī' with one more pāda added to 'Gāyatrī.'

8. जगती गततमं छन्दः। जलचरगतिर्वा जल्गल्यमानोऽसृजदिति च ब्राह्मणम्।

jagati gatamaṁ chandaḥ jalacaragatirvā jalgalyamāyo'sṛjaditi ca brāhmaṇam.[77]

'Jagati' is the last metre. It has a flow like water

[74]. *ibid.* 6.31 (123).
[75]. *ibid.* 7.12.
[76]. *ibid.*7.12
[77]. *ibid.* 7.13.

waves. It was enchanted while pushing water with hands. This is the view of the Brāhmaṇas.'

9. अथापि ब्राह्मणं भवति 'अग्निः सर्वा देवता'।

athāpi brāhmaṇam bhavati agniḥ sarvā devatā.[78]

'Also the Brāhmaṇas had it as all the deities (natural forces) are manifestation of agni (energy).'

10. अथापि ब्राह्मणं भवति अग्निर्वा इतो वृष्टिं समीरयति धामच्छद् दिवि भूत्वा वर्षति मरुतः सृष्टां वृष्टिं नयन्ति। यदा खलु वासवादित्योऽग्निं रश्मिभिः पर्यावर्ततेऽथ वर्षतीति।

athāpi brāhmaṇam bhavatyagnirvā ito vṛṣṭiṁ samīrayati dhāmacchad divi bhūtvā varṣati marutaḥ sṛṣṭāṁ vṛṣṭiṁ nayanti. yadā khalu vāsāvādityo agniṁ raśmibhiḥ paryāvartate' tha varṣatīti. [79]

'There is Brāhmaṇa: Agni stimulates rain from here. The clouds precipitate from the sky. Maruta brings the rains down. The Sun vaporizes waters into the sky and the rain takes place.'

यथो एतद् ब्राह्मणं भवतीति—बहुभक्तिवादिनि हि ब्राह्मणानि भवन्ति—पृथिवी वैश्वानरः संवत्सरो वैश्वानरो ब्राह्मणो वैश्वानर इति।

yatho etad brāhmaṇaṁ bhavatīti bahubhaktivādīni hi brāhmaṇāni bhavanti pṛthivī vaiśvānaraḥ saṁvatsaro vaiśvānaro brāhmaṇo vaiśvānara iti. [80]

'As the Brāhmaṇas had it: pṛthivī is vaiśvānara; saṁvatsara is vaiśvānara; Brāhmaṇa is vaiśvānara; etc. The Brāhmaṇas speaks of may identifications of one and the same object.'

11. यदस्य दिवि तृतीयं तदादित्य इति हि ब्राह्मणम्।

yadasya divi tṛtīyaṁ tadāditya iti hi brāhmaṁam.[81]

---

78. *ibid.* 7.17.
79. *ibid.* 7.24.
80. *ibid.* 7.24
81. *ibid.* 7.28.

'The third form of agni (energy) which exists in the light space is called āditya, according to some of the *Brāhmaṇas.*'

12. अथातः आप्रियः। आप्रियः कस्मादाप्नोतिः प्रीणातेर्वा। आप्रीभिराप्रीणातीति च ब्राह्मणम्।

athāta āprīyaḥ kasmādānoteḥ prīnāterva āprībhirāprīṇātīti ca brāhmaṇam. [82]

'Now we shall take the word 'āpriyaḥ'. 'Āpriyaḥ' means that which obtains or satisfies. The Brāhmaṇas also say, 'With the help of 'Āprī Ṛcās' he satisfies the people.'

All the aforementioned citations from the Brāhmaṇas clearly indicates the subject matter of Brāhmaṇas. Earlier Brāhmaṇas were devoid of any type of ritualism or ritualistic formulae. They consisted only of the explanatory statements. Those explanatory statements were often called as 'vidhivākyas'. For instance, Śabarswami in the *Mantrādhikaraṇa* while commenting on *vidhiśabdācca* described explanatory statements of the Brāhmaṇas as 'vidhi'.

मन्त्रव्याख्यानरूपो ब्राह्मणगतः शब्दः 'विधि' शब्द इत्युच्यते।

Mantravyākhyārupo brāhmaṇagataḥ śabdo vidhiśabda ityucyate. [83]

In fact, only those statements composed the real character of the early Brāhmaṇas.

In support of the author's contention that only the explanatory statements which later came to be known as 'arthavāda' were known as 'vidhi' at the earliest stage, Sāyaṇa's observation on the *VS.* 3.18. may be cited. He explains as under:

मन्त्रव्याख्यानरूपो ब्राह्मणगतः शब्दः 'विधि' शब्द इत्युच्यते। स

---

82 . *ibid.* 8.84.
83 . *Jaiminīya Mimāṁsā Sūtra* (JMS) 1.2.5.3.

चैवाम्नाये शतं हिमाः शतं वर्षाणि जीव्यास्म इत्येव एतदाह (श.ब्रा. .3.4.21) शतं हिमाः (यजुर्वेद, 3.18) इत्येतद् व्याख्येय मन्त्रस्य प्रतीकं अवशिष्टं तु तस्य तात्पर्य व्याख्यानम्।

Mantravyākhānarūpo brāhmaṇagataḥ śabdo vidhiśabda ityucyate. sa caivāmnāyate śataṁ himāḥ śataṁ vaıṣāṇi jīvyāsma ityeva etadāha. (*Ś.Br.* 2.3.4.21) *śataṁ himāḥ* (*VS.* 3.18) *ityetad vyākhyeyaMantrasya pratīkam avaśiṣ ṭaṁ tu tasya tātparyavyākhyānam.* [84]

'Statements of the Brāhmaṇas explaining the Mantras are called 'vidhis'. The same is documented as follows. In the context of the Mantra *'śataṁ himāḥ',* the Brāhmaṇa says, let me live for hundred years. here '*śataṁ himāḥ*' is the portion of the Mantra to be explained and the rest is its explanation.'

From the above observation of Sāyaṇa, it is crystal clear that the term 'vidhi' was applied to the explanatory notes of the Brāhmaṇas.

Development of ritualism in the Brāhmaṇas

With the passage of time, later heirs of the various Vedic schools added more and more explanatory material to what they already inherited in tradition. Since Yajña or Deva Yajña was the part and parcel of the Vedic life (Author 1995: 1). The later heirs started associating the Brāhmaṇas with the Yajña being performed by them daily. This was so done that the real import of the Vedas may not be forgotten being repeated day by day in course of daily Yajña. Thus the Vedic Mantras were explained in the light of Yajña, or Agnihotra, or Deva Yajña. This added the new dimensions to the Brāhmaṇic tradition. Earlier Agnihotra was used to be performed in order to augment the deficient powers of various deities in nature. But, by this time Agnihotra was performed in order to unravel the various mysteries of Brahman, the consciousness, and nature narrated in the Mantras. For instance, the *Ś.Br.*

---

84 . *Ṛgveda Bhāṣya-Bhūmikā*, P. 24.

talks about the Agnihotra which could expound/explain the actual concept of Brahman to Śauceya.

शौचेयो ह प्राचीनयोग्य उद्दालकमारूणिमाजगाम ब्रह्मोद्यम् अग्निहोत्रं विविदिषिष्यामि इति।

Śuceyo ha prācinayogya uddālakam ārūṇimājagāma brahmodyam agnihotraṁ vividıṣıṣyāmi iti.[85]

We come across a reference in the *Ś.Br.* where Darśa Pūrṇamāsa Yajñas (being performed on Amāvasyā and Pūrṇamāsī) and Cāturmāsya Yajñas (being performed during the rainy season) are depicted as having, in addition to their actual purpose of Devayajña, also to serve the purpose of Ātmayajña (i.e. self-realization). (Note: Devayajñas were the yajñas that were performed daily at dawn and twilight hours, on Full-mood day, in dark fortnight, in the beginning, and at the end of each changing season, so that the natural forces may be coordinated to suit the requirements of living beings on the Earth) [86]

प्रजापतिर्ह चातुर्मास्यैरात्मानं विदधे।

prajāpatirha cāturmāsyairātmānaṁ vidadhe [87]

Sāyaṇa's commentary is also noteworthy here. According to him 'Just as twofold objects of the Darśa and Pūrṇamāsa Yajñas have been revealed. Cāturmasya Yajña is also performed with twofold objectives. In order to perform it for self-realization, the division of body parts is made through the ākhyānya that follows.'

The above-cited fact points out that Agnihotra that was performed earlier in order to co-ordinate natural forces, later came to be performed to explain the Mantras. The significance of the Mantras was told with the acts and figures (combinedly known as rituals) of the allegorical Yajñas.

---

85 . 11.5.3.1.
86 . For detail see, author (1995 : 1)
87 . *Ś.Br.* 11.5.2.1.

The *Śāṁkhāyana Āraṇyaka* also tells us that the Agnihotra was not performed earlier in order to explain the significance of the Mantras.

तद्ध स्मैतत्पूर्वे विद्वांसोऽग्निहोत्रं न जुह्वांचक्रे।

taddha smaitatpūrve vidvāṁso'gnihotraṁ na juhvāñcakruḥ [88]

Since those Yajñas were not mandatory. They were only the means of understanding the actual import of the Vedas. This is why earlier Yājñikas at the time of expounding the methods of various Yajñas for the understanding of Vedārtha (meaning of the Vedas) also specified that performing Yajña or knowing its method thoroughly (*ya u cainaṁ Veda*) was equally fruitful in understanding the real import of the Vedas. For instance, the *Śāṁkhāyana Āraṇyaka* had it as:

यज्ञानुष्ठाने तच्च यज्ञं तत्त्वतो ज्ञाने सममेव फलं दर्शितम्।

yajñānuṣṭhāne tacca Yajñaṁ tattvato jñāne samameva phalaṁ darśitam. [89]

The later development of this ritualism in the Brāhmaṇas is also supported by the following statements of various texts.

According to the *Vāyupurāṇa:*

अथ त्रेतायुगमुखे यज्ञस्यासीत् प्रवर्तनम्।

atha tretā yugamukhe yajñasyāsīt pravartanam [90]

Rituals prevailed only in the beginning of the Tretāyuga.

According to the *Mahābharta*:

त्रेतायुगे विधिस्त्वेष यज्ञं न कृतयुगे।

tretāyuge vidhis tveṣa yajñāṁ na kṛtayuge. [91]

---

[88]. 4.5.
[89]. *ibid.*
[90]. 57.89.

'The Yajña was applied as a means of Vedārtha only in the Tretāyuga and not in the Satyayuga'

Also *Muṇḍakopaniṣad* had it as:

तदेतत् सत्यं मन्त्रेषु कर्माणि कवयोः

यान्यपश्यन्स्तानि त्रेतायां बहुधा संततानि।

tadetat satyaṁ mantreṣu karmāṇi kavayoḥ
yānyapaśyaṁstāni tretāyāṁ bahudhā santatāni [92]

'This is true that the significance of Mantras was not considered in the application of rituals earlier. But by the time of Tretāyuga, the ritualism developed exorbitantly.'

With the development of the various rituals for the understanding of the Vedārtha, the definition of the Brāhmaṇas also changed. For example, the term 'vidhi' that was earlier used for the explanatory statements, now came to be used for the prescription of some rituals.

तत्र विधिः प्रयोजनवद् अर्थविधानेनऽर्थवान्।

tatra vidhiḥ prayojanavad artha vidhānenā'rthvān. [93]

However, for the explanatory statements, the term was coined as 'arthavāda'.

With this, the definition of Brāhmaṇas also changed. It came to be as:

कर्मचोदना ब्राह्मणानि।

karma codanā brāhmaṇāni (Āpastamba). [94]

'The Brāhmaṇas prescribes various rituals.'

Later Yājñikās

The later Yājñikā-s unmindful of the fact that the origin

---

91. 23.232.
92. 1.2.1.
93. Āpadeva, *Mim. Nya. Prakaraṇa, Vidhi nirupaṇa*
94. Yajña Paribhāṣa, 1.1.32.

and development of various Yajñas took place for the explanation of the process of creation described in the Vedas took the Yajñas only for rituals. So they separated the ritual portion of the Brāhmaṇas from the explanatory notes. Consequent upon which *vidhyātmaka Brāhmaṇas*, i.e. ritual pron Brāhmaṇas were compiled separately under the caption *Śrauta Sūtras*.

On the other hand, to oppose the yājñika fundamentalism, there arose a new lobby of scholars who deadly opposed the yājñika karmakāṇḍa, the ritualism and favoured arthavāda. They also forget the purpose of arthvāda and took it only for jñanakāṇḍa. So, they compiled the arthvadātmaka Brāhmaṇas separately under the caption of Āraṇyakas and later as Upaniṣads. Both the Karmakāṇḍa and Jñānakāṇḍa emerged as the rival forces. Karmakaṇdins are met with opposing Jñānakaṇḍins and Jñānakaṇḍins are found opposing Karmakāṇḍins.

Still later Yājñikā-s (ritualists) seem to have developed a craze for rituals. They evolved an unrestricted number of rituals. It, however, became an uphill task for them to find out the appropriate Mantras as could be fitted into the newly evolved rituals. Consequently, the priests were hard-pressed to pick up such Mantras as could be recited at the performance of such later rituals as were unconnected with them. Since the priests were not aware of the real import of Mantras, they employed Mantras, without caring for the sense and context at the performance of a ritual, on the basis of the slightest or superficial similarity of a sound or the sense of ritual and the Mantra. This craze of the priests led to the indiscriminate employment of Mantras at the performance of their newly evolved rituals that sometimes one and the same Mantra is found employed for various opposite rituals.

For instance, the Ṛgvedic Mantra 10.53.8. also occurring in the *AV.* 12.2.26; *VS.* 3510., is on the one hand prescribed in *Kāt. S.S.* 21.4.21; and *Āśv. G.S.* 4.6.13. for the performance of a funeral rite, on the other hand, the same Mantra is employed in *Āśv. G.S.* 1.8.2.3.; *Sāṅkh. G.S.* 1.15.18. and *Kaṭh. G.S.* 26.12. when the newly wedded couple crosses a river in a boat.

Significance of the Brāhmaṇas in the Vedic Interpretation

The role of the Brāhmaṇas in the interpretation of the Vedas is very significant. The explanatory statements (earlier known as vidhi śabdas and later as arthvādas) of the Brāhmaṇas, as discussed earlier, are the direct meaning of the Vedas passed on to us by the original seers. Earlier, rituals were also evolved to explain the real import of the Vedas in the light of Agnihotra being performed then regularly by the inheritors of the Vedas. This is why Yāska while justifying the objections of Kautsa calls the Brāhmaṇas consisting of such rituals as 'uditānuvāda' or 'expressions of the already expressed meaning' of the Mantras. For instance, he had it as:

ब्राह्मणेन रूपसम्पन्नाः विधियन्ते इति उदितानुवादः स भवति।

brāhmaṇena rūp saṁpannāḥ vidhiyante iti uditānuvādaḥ sa bhavanti.

'Rituals of the Brāhmaṇas are expressions of the already expressed meaning of the Vedas.'

In the view of the later commentators, the Brāhmaṇas are essential for the interpretation of the Vedic *Mantras.* Veṅkaṭamādhava in his *Ṛgarthadīpkā* attaches more importance to the Brāhmaṇas so far as the interpretation of the Vedas is concerned than to the Grammar and the Nirukta. According to him, the unknown and doubtful meanings of the Mantras can be ascertained well at the hands of the scholars who are well versed in the Brāhmaṇas than those whose study is confined only to the Nirukta and Grammar. The scholars who excel in Nirukta and grammar are able to understand only the quarter part of the Saṁhitā, but the scholars excelled in the Brāhmaṇas know the style and diction of words and are able to know the complete meaning of the Saṁhitā, e.g.

> अस्माभिस्त्विह मन्त्राणामर्थः प्रत्येकमुच्यते। येऽज्ञाता ये च संदिग्धास्तासां वृद्धेषु निर्णय निरुक्त–व्याकरणयोंरासीद्येषां परिश्रमः। अथ ये ब्राह्मणार्थानां विवेक्तारः कृत्श्रमाः शब्दरीतिं विजानन्ति ते सर्वां कथयन्त्यपि।
>
> *asmābhistviha mantraṇāmarthaḥ pratyekamucyate ye'jjñātā ye ca sandigdhās tāṣāṁ vṛddheṣu nirṇaya nirukta-vyākaraṇayor-āsīdyeṣāṁ pariśramaḥ.*
> *atha ye brāhmaṇārthānām vivektāraḥ kṛtśramāḥ śabdarītiṁ vijānanti te sarvām kathayantyapi.* [95]

In fact, all other schools came into being later, such as Nairukta, Naidāna, Privrājaka, and Aitihāsika, etc. in a way or other owe much to the Brāhmaṇas.

---

95. *Ṛgarthadīpikā*, 8.1.1-10.

The Nairukta School of the Vedic Interpretation

The Nairuktas also attempted to interpret the Vedic words on the basis of their derivative connotation. It is known as an etymological or Nairukta method of Vedic interpretation. The Niruktas are also owed to the Brahmaṇas for the origin of their method of interpretation. Yāska's *Nirukta* is the last and best representative of this school of interpretation. Yāska (Kali 400, i.e. c. 28 century BC) also refers by name to about a dozen authorities on Nirukta, the science of etymology, viz., Aupamanyava, Sākapūṇi, Gālava (last century of 28th Dvāpara i.e. 56 years before 28 Kali, i.e. c. 32 century BC), Maudgalya (28th Dvāpara), Āgrāyaṇa (28th Dvāpara), Kātthakya (28th Dvāpara), Krauṣṭuki (28th Dvāpara), Aurṇavābha (28th Dvāpara), Audumbarāyaṇa (28th Kali 94, i.e. c. 31 century BC), Gārgya (last century of 28th Dvāpara i.e. 56 years before 28 Kali, i.e. c. 32 century BC), and Śākṭāyana (28th Kali 44, i.e. c. 31 century BC). Besides, he also refers to the etymologists in general as Nairuktāḥ. The works of all the predecessors of Yāska seem to have been irretrievably lost, and we do not know anything about them except stray references to their names. In order to understand the development of the Nirukta in proper perspective, it is essential to have an idea of the Saṁhitā pāṭha and padapāṭ ha of the *RV.* and the other the Vedas. The Nirukti or etymology was an attempt to invent the actual intent, concept, or background within which the particular word or words originated.

The word 'Nirukta' literally means 'explanation' or 'etymological interpretation of a word'. The *Nighaṇṭu* worked as the basis of the explanations or etymologies given in the *Nirukta*. In other words, it can be stated that Nirukta is an explanation of the Vedic words listed in the *Nighaṇṭu*, or one can say that it is a commentary on the

Nighaṇṭu as admitted by Yāska himself in the very beginning of the *Nirukta*. Since it is the only work of its kind available at present, the title 'Nirukta' now means the Vedic commentary composed by Yāska. The *Nirukta* which consists of twelve chapters and an appendix is one of the systematic attempts to interpret Vedic words, passages, and deities of the *RV*. The *Nirukta*, in fact, is a key to decode the scientific meaning of the Vedas.

The first chapter which is introductory in nature deals with the scope and importance of Nirukta; and in the course of the discussion, Yāska brings in several linguistic questions of a general nature and presents a systematic debate on them. For instance, the following controversial issues are debated by Yāska in the first chapter:

(a). Whether speech exists in the speech organs only;

(b). Whether the prepositions have any independent meanings of their own;

(c). Whether all the nouns have been derived from verbs; and

(d). Whether the Vedic words have any meanings. The views expressed by Yāska on such controversial issues are rational and reflect his vast learning.

At the beginning of the second chapter, Yāska enunciates the principles of etymology. First of all, he lays down the general principle that to know the intended sense of a Vedic word, one should derive it in conformity with its regular accent, grammatical form, and radical modification. However, when the accent, grammatical form, and radical modification of a word are irregular, its derivation becomes difficult. In such a situation, Yāska's advice is that one should etymologize in accordance with the meaning of the word on the basis of a similarity of common usage or of even a syllable or a letter but one must never give up the attempt to etymologize. In this connection, Yāska cautions an etymologist against placing undue reliance on grammar, for the usages of words are obscure. Therefore, one should interpret grammatical affixes in keeping with the sense of words. Yāska advises an etymologist to take due notice of important phonetic phenomena, such as syncope, metathesis, anaptyxis, haplology, assimilation, etc., at the time of derivation. The most important principle of etymology enunciated by Yāska is that words should be derived in accordance with their contextual meaning and that no attempt should be made to derive single words, i.e., words taken out of context.

Commencing with the fifth section of the second chapter up to the end of the third chapter, Yāska takes up a systematic derivation of some selected synonyms listed in the first three chapters of the *Nighaṇṭu.* First of all, he mentions the exact number of synonyms listed in a particular section of the *Nighaṇṭu* and then gives the derivation of a few important words of the section. In order to illustrate the Vedic usage of the words under discussion, he cites a Vedic passage and paraphrases it explaining the meaning of difficult words occurring in it.

The obscure Vedic words compiled in the fourth chapter of the *Nighanṭu* have been systematically explained by Yāska in the fourth, fifth, and sixth chapters of his work in the manner explained above.

Chapters seven to twelve of the *Nirukta* have been devoted to the discussion of various aspects of the Vedic deities listed in the fifth chapter of the *Nighaṇṭu.* At the beginning of the seventh chapter of the *Nirukta,* Yāska attempts the dentition of a deity (devatā), enumerates various types of the Ṛgvedic verses according to their subject matter, and presents different viewpoints on the question of ascertaining the deity of those Mantras where no deity has been specifically mentioned. Then Yāska discusses the nature, number, form, and place of operation and mutual relationship of Vedic deities.

From the fourteenth section of the seventh chapter up to

the end of the twelfth chapter, Yāska takes up for discussion the place of operation, nature, and etymology of Vedic deities in the same order in which their names are listed in the fifth chapter of the *Nighaṇṭu.* In order to illustrate his viewpoint, he cites verses from the *RV.* and explains the verses and obscure words occurring in them in the manner described above. The thirteenth chapter of the *Nirukta* which is called Pariśiṣṭa, 'appendix', is not Yāska's composition because it contains the words '*namo Yāskāya*' at the end. Besides, the style of explanation and the contents of the 13th chapter also distinguish it from the preceding twelve chapters. Moreover, since Yāska's commentary on the *Nighaṇṭu* concludes with the l2th chapter, there is no *raison d'etre* for the I3th chapter. It is thus obvious that the 13th chapter which is found in some Manuscripts divided into two chapters was appended to the *Nirukta* at a later date.

In the twelve chapters of the *Nirukta*, Yāska explains nearly 600 verses of the *RV.* and suggests the etymology of about 'I300' words. Yāska's explanation of the Vedic verses is rational and free from supernatural elements because following in the footsteps of the Nairuktas he endeavours to explain the natural phenomena underlying the names occurring in the Veda and thus offers a scientific interpretation of Vedic gods. For instance, with regard to the interpretation of Vṛtra, Yāska (2.16) quotes with approbation the view of the Nairuktas that Vṛtra is a cloud, and elucidates the same with the remarks that the phenomenon of rain takes place due to discharging of negative and positive currents in the clouds, or negatively charged clouds with the positive earth and that the Vedic descriptions of fights between lndra (negative electric charge in clouds) and Vṛtra (positively charged clouds or earth) are metaphorical. See for example

तत्को वृत्रः। मेघ इति नैरुक्ताः। त्वाष्ट्रोऽसुर इत्यैतिहासिकाः। अपां च ज्योतिषश्च मिश्रीभावकर्मणो वर्षकर्म जायते। तत्र उपमार्थेन युद्धवर्णा भवन्ति।

tatko vṛtraḥ. Medha iti nairuktāḥ. tvâṣṭro asura iti aitihāsikāḥ. apāṁ cha jyotiṣaśca mıṣribhāvakarmaṇo vaıṣakarma jāyate. Tatra upamārthena yudhvarṇā bhavanti.

What is Vṛtra? In view of Nairuktas, Vṛtra is a cloud. According to Aitihāsikas, vṛtra is an asura, son of Tvaṣṭā. When clouds are charged, rain takes place.

He alludes to the use of metaphorical expressions in the Veda (2.16). Yāska was able to discover the scientific meaning of the Vedic deities. His following remarks with regard to them are illuminating and provide a key to the correct interpretation of the Veda:

महाभाग्याद् देवताया एक आत्मा बहुधा स्तूयते। नि. 7.4

mahābhāgyād devatāyā eka ātmā bahudhā stūyate

On account of various qualities of the deity (devatā), one and the same deity is known by various names.

एकस्य आत्मनः अन्ये देवाः प्रत्यंगानि भवन्ति। नि. 7.4

Ekasya ātmanaḥ anye devāḥ pratyaṅgāni bhavanti

The other gods associated with a particular deity are but his parts. That is, they cannot be separated from or are not different from their parent deity.

अपि च सत्त्वानां प्रकृतिभूमभिर्ऋषयः स्तुवन्तीत्याहुः। नि. 7.4

api cha sattvānāṁ prakṛtibhāmir ṛṣayaḥ stuvantītyāhuḥ.

Moreover, other experts say that because of the plurality of the intrinsic nature of deities, seers praise them variously.

प्रकृतिसार्वनाम्याच्च। नि. 7.4

prakṛti-sārvanāmyācca

All names of gods in various spaces (observer space, intermediate space, and light space) refer to their presiding deity.

For example, Agni, Indra & Vāyu, and Āditya are the presiding deities of observer space, intermediate space, and light space respectively. If we find mention of other gods in these three spaces, they will refer to their presiding deity itself. They don't have an independent existence. They are subservient to their main deity or presiding deity.

According to Nairuktas the Vedic deities/gods (devatās) are not historical personalities but are natural forces. That is why they are born from each other. Had they been historical persons, they could not have born from each other. For example, he observes:

इतेरजन्मानो भवन्ति। नि. 7.4

itaretara janmāno bhavanti

The Devas/gods are born from each other.

To illustrate it, matter particles (gods in observer space) are born from energy (Agni) and energy is born from matter particles (Devas/gods).

इतरेतरप्रकृतयः। नि. 7.4

itaretara prakṛtayaḥ

They are the primary source of each other.

For example, energy (Agni) is the source of matter particles and matter particles (Devas/gods in observer space) are the source of energy.

On the question as to why do these deities take birth, the reply is that they are born because they execute specific functions in materialising the process of creation. In this regard Yāska, observes as under:

कर्मजन्मानः। नि. 7.4

karma-janmānaḥ

They owe their birth to their specific functions.

One may ask another question as to how do they bear? The reply is that the Vedic gods are not born like human beings from their parents, but are born automatically themselves whenever they are required to discharge their respective functions to execute the process of creation. For example, in a process to maintain a delicate balance between energy and matter for the sustenance of this universe, anti-matter particles are born automatically to annihilate their existing matter particles. Similarly, moving clouds are automatically become negatively charged in order to discharge rain by discharging with the positively charged clouds or the earth. Here Yāska's observation is noteworthy-

आत्मजन्मानः। नि. 7.4

ātmajanmānaḥ

The Vedic Devas/gods are born automatically.

Not only this, Yāska makes a clarification about the chariots, horses weapons, and arrows of gods mentioned in the Vedas. Since the Vedic gods are not living historical personalities, how to interpret the chariots, horses, weapons, and arrows associated with them in the Vedic Mantras. Yāska dispels this doubt and observes that the chariots, weapons, and horses of Devas or gods mentioned in the Vedas are nothing but gods themselves are their own chariots, weapons, and horses. So, their horses, chariots, etc. cannot be taken separate entities from them. According to him,

आत्मैवेषां रथो भवति । आत्माश्वः। आत्मायुधम्। आत्मेषवः। आत्मा सर्वं देवस्य। नि. 7.4

ātmaiveṣāṁ ratho bhavati. ātmāśvaḥ. ātmāyudham. ātmā sarva devasya.

The Devas are themselves their chariot, horse, and weapons. Deva itself is every thing associated with it.

Thus we find that Yaska's interpretation is most systematic and scientific. He gives us a real clue to interpreting the astronomical phenomenon mentioned in the Vedas. No other interpreter of ancient India has displayed so much rationality in his approach to the problem of Vedic interpretation. Yāska may be described as scientific in his approach, notwithstanding his remote antiquity, surprisingly modern.

Here it cannot be gainsaid that the Vedic language is highly developed and the words used in the Vedas very carefully express thoughts inherent in them in a poetic style marked with metaphors. The correct etymology of a word often provides a clue to its real intended meaning. For instance, the Vedic seers employ the word 'jāra' in the following phrases in a poetical style to denote the sun:

स्वसुर्जार, जार उषसाम्, अपां जारः।

Svasur jāra, jāra uṣasām, apāṁ jāraḥ

According to the popular sense of words, it would mean -'Paramour of his sister', 'paramour of dawns', and 'paramour of waters' respectively.' But if the word 'jāra' is interpreted as 'consumer', 'jārayitā', following Yāska's derivation, from root 'jṛ' 'to consume', the meaning would be rational, scientific, and linguistically sound. In this case, the meaning would be read as - 'Sun is the consumer of dawn, consumer of waters and consumer of his sister 'dawn'.

Thus the main advantage of the etymological method of interpretation is that it helps us to distinguish the original radical meaning of a word from its conventional meaning in those cases in which a word is yielding two meanings. It is evident from an analysis of Vedic usages that the use of *double entendre* often comes across. Alluding to this tendency of the Vedic language, the Brāhmaṇas observe that the Devas/gods love recondite speech and abhor direct statements.

परोक्षप्रिया इव हि देवाः प्रत्यक्ष द्विषः।

Prokṣapriyā iva hi devāḥ pratyakṣa dvıṣaḥ

Here it would be unwise if a reference to the *Nighaṇṭu* is by-passed. As told earlier that the *Nighaṇṭu* worked as a basis for Nairuktas. So, it is essential to take a brief note of the *Nighaṇṭu.*

The Nighaṇṭu

After Padapātha, the *Nighaṇṭu* occupies an important place in the annals of linguistic study of the Vedas and may be termed as the first lexicographical attempt in the world. The term 'Nighaṇṭu' signifies a collection and classification of important words occurred in the Vedas so that their decoding from the point of their significance is made easy. The *Nighaṇṭu,* or 'Samāmnāya' as it is called in the beginning of the *Nirukta,* is divided into five chapters and is therefore also called *Pañchādhyāyī.* The first three chapters contain classified groups of synonyms. For instance, the synonyms of the earth (meaning observer space, or planets) are listed in the first section of the first chapter and those of antrikṣa (meaning intermediate space, or atmosphere) and dyau (meaning light space or celestial sphere) in the third and the fourth sections respectively. There is some sort of a principle discernible in the arrangement of synonyms in the first three chapters. So the first chapter deals with physical objects and natural phenomena such as earth, air, water, clouds, dawn, day, and night. The synonyms collected in the second chapter relate to man, his limbs, qualities, actions, and achievements. The synonymous words collected in the third chapter deal with abstract qualities such as heaviness, lightness etc., according to Dr. L. Sarup. But there are so many exceptions also. The first three chapters containing Vedic synonyms are regarded to constitute the Naighaṭuka Kāṇḍa. The fourth chapter which is styled as Naigama Kāṇḍa contains a list of such Vedic words whose meaning is not easy to understand and needs to be explained. Such words have been listed under 'pada-nāma'. These 'padas' are nothing but the scientific and technical terms which need to be defined and cannot be translated. The fifth chapter called 'Daivata Kāṇḍa' is a glossary of the names of Vedic deities.

As regards the authorship of the *Nighaṇṭu*, it may be stated that it was the effort of many generations of Nairuktas to collect Vedic words so as to make their encoding easy. It is confirmed by the statement of Yāska when he says at the outset of the *Nirukta* that the Samāmnāya, Nighaṇṭu which had already been compiled and needs to be explained.

The Other Ancient Schools of Vedic Interpretation

In addition to the three major schools of Vedic interpretation discussed earlier, some other significant systems of Vedic interpretation existed in ancient India. Among such schools of Vedic interpretation, the Parivrājaka school of Vedic interpretation, which may be called the Ādhyātmika (Mystic) School of Vedic interpretation, figures prominently, because it has got a long history and a traditional base. Besides, Naidānas also attempted in their own way the interpretation of certain Vedic Mantras as attested by the *Nirukta*, the *Mahābhāṣya*, the *Baudhāyana Dharma Sūtra*, etc.

The Parivrājaka (Mystic) School of Vedic Interpretation

The Parivrājaka school of Vedic interpretation referred

to by Yāska (2.8) may be regarded as representing those scholars who attempt a Ādhyātmika (mystic) interpretation of the Vedas. According to this school of exegesis, Ādhyātma (mysticism) is the most prominent import of the Vedic Mantras.

The earliest specimens of mystic interpretation of the Vedas are met within the Brāhmaṇas as well as in the Āraṇyakas and the Upaniṣads embodied in them. The followers of this school of Vedic exegesis attempted the mystic interpretation of Vedic deities and Yajñas also. Several instances of such interpretations are found in the Brāhmaṇas, the Āraṇyakas, and the Upaniṣads. For instance, Mitra and Varuṇa are interpreted as inhalation (Prāṇa) and exhalation (Apāna) respectively in the prose portion of the *Tait. S.* and in many Brāhmaṇas. But such Ādhyātmika (mystic) explanations offered in the Brāhmaṇas have other parallel interpretations. For instance, the god Indra has been interpreted in the Brāhmaṇas as speech, inhalation (Prāṇa), mind, the Sun, Vāyu, etc. Yāska (7.24) refers to this tendency of the Brāhmaṇas as

बहुभक्तिवादीनि हि ब्राह्मणानि भवन्ति।

bahubhakti vādīni hi brāhmaṇāni bhavanti.

> That is Brāhmaṇas speak of various parallel meanings based upon various characteristics of one and the same deity.

Among the mystic explanations of Vedic Śrauta Yajñas, that of the Aśvamedha is worth noticing, for the *Taittirīya Saṁhitā* (7.5.25), the *Śatapatha Brāhmaṇa* (10.6.4), and the *Bṛhadāraṇyaka Upaniṣad* (1.1) interpret the Aśva (horse) of Aśvamedha Yajña as a cosmic force identical with the world through an allegory. Accordingly, the Dawn is the head of the Aśva, the Sun its eye, the Wind its breath, Agni Vaiśvānara its Open mouth, the Moon its ear, quarters its feet, the sky its back, the air its belly, the earth under-part of its belly, the intermediate quarters its ribs, the seasons its limbs, the months and half-months its joints, the day and night its winking, the stars its bones, the clouds its flesh, the sand its intestinal food, the rivers its bowels, the mountains its liver and lungs, the herbs and trees its hair, the rising sun its forepart, the setting sun its hind part, the lightning its yawning, the thundering its whinning, and the speech is its voice. The Brāhmaṇas emphasise that a wise man who meditates upon the real nature of the 'Aśva' identical with the cosmic force understands the real Aśvamedha."

We witness in the Āraṇyakas and the Upaniṣads an upsurge of the tendency of attempting a mystic interpretation of Vedic Śrauta Yajñas, which in its turn led to the mystic interpretation of Vedic verses. For instance, the fifth Prapāṭhaka of the *Taittirīya Āraṇyaka* suggests the mystic explanation of the oblation given in the fire in the first Pravargya ceremony introductory to the Soma Yāga. The *Taittirīya Āraṇyaka* (5.8.12) asserts that in fact, Agni (fire) here stands for inhalation (Prāṇa).

इन्द्रतमेऽग्नौ इति आह। प्राणो वै इन्द्रतमोऽग्निः।

indratame'gnau iti āha. prāṇo vai indratamo'gniḥ.

In the *Nārāyaṇa Upaniṣad* comprised in the *Taittirīya Āraṇyaka* (10.64) some important yāgas, their constituent ceremonies and materials have been symbolically and mystically interpreted for a knower of truth who has renounced the world. For such a person his own self is the Yajamāna (performer of Yajña), faith (śraddhā) his wife, body the samidhā, chest the altar, hair the kuśa grass, heart the yūpa (post of Yajña), desire the clarified butter, anger the paśu (animal) to be sacrificed in the Yajña, and austerity is the fire of Yajña. Self-control is the slayer of the paśu (animal). Speech is his dakṣīṇā of Yajña. Inhalation (Prāṇa) is his Udgatr priest, eye his Adhvaryu priest, mind his Brahman priest, and the ear is his Agnīdha priest. His whole life is an act of consecration. His food is the oblation to be offered to the Yajña, and his drink is the Soma–draught. Day and night are his full moon

(Paurṇamāsa Yajña) and new-moon (Darśa Yajña). Half-months and months are his Chāturmāsya Yajñas. Seasons are his Paśu Yāgas. Years are the series of his days of Yajña (aharganas). His life is a great Soma yāga called Sarva-Vedasa in which the entire property is given away, and his death is the final bath of Yajña called Avabhṛtha. This is an Agnihotra lasting throughout life.

The tenth chapter of the *Sāṅkhāyana Āraṇyaka* also contains a symbolical and spiritual interpretation of the Agnihotra. Similarly the *Chhāndogya Upaniṣad* (3, 16-17) symbolically describes a person's entire life as a Yajña. Following the Āraṇyakas and the Upaniṣads, the *Bhagavadgītā* 4, 23-33, too, offers a symbolical and spiritual explanation of Vedic Yajñas.

In pursuance of the mystic interpretation of the Vedic verses and Yajñas some Āraṇyakas and Upaniṣads regard breath, speech, etc., as the subject-matter of certain Vedic verses. For instance, the *Aitareya Āraṇyaka* (2.16) and the *Jaiminīya Upaniṣad Brāhmaṇa* (3.6.9.2-5) regard Prāṇa as the deity of the *RV*. 1.164.31 and accordingly offer its mystic interpretation. Similarly, the Rgvedic verses 1.164.38 and 10. 1 14.4 are also interpreted by the *Aitareya Āraṇyaka* (2.1.8) as connected with the description of breath. According to the *Jaiminīya Upaniṣad Brāhmaṇa* (3.35.1-8), the Ṛgvedic verses 10.177.1-2 relate to Prāṇa. In the supplementary portion (Chapters 13 and 14) of the *Nirukta* the mystic interpretation of nearly twenty Vedic verses has been suggested, and most of the later commentators and scholars also favour their mystic interpretation.

The ancient scholars who suggested the mystic interpretation of Vedic verses were called Ātmavids, Ātmavādins, or Ātmapravādas, the Parivrājakas being ones among them. Thus the Ādhyātmika (mystic/metaphysical) interpretation of the Vedas has been one of the primary interpretations of the Vedas, followed by Ādhidaivika (astronomical) and Ādhibhautika (material and sociological) interpretations.

Naidāna School of Vedic Interpretation

The word Nidāna has been used in the sense of the primary cause of the visualisation of Vedic verses. Naidānas were those who used to interpret Vedic verses on the basis of the primary cause of the visualisation of the Vedic verses. Yāska refers to the views of the Naidānas with regard to the etymologies of the words Syāla (6.9) and Sāman (7.12). In his commentary on the Nirukta (6.9), Durgāchārya explains *Naidānāḥ* as *Nidānavidaḥ*, i.e. those who are expert in Nidāna (the primary cause of the visualisation of Vedic verses). Elsewhere in his commentary Durgāchārya employs the term Nidāna in the sense of the primary cause of Vedic verses to explain ltihāsa and thus makes Nidāna as the basis of ltihāsa. Therefore in the opinion of Durgāchārya, the meaning of the word Naidāna is very near to that of Aitihāsikas but is not identical because Yāska's separate and distinct mention of *Naidānāḥ* and *Aitihāsikaḥ* points to the difference in their meanings. It leads us to the inference that the Naidāna system of Vedic interpretation was definitely distinct from that of the Aitihasikas. The point of subtle difference was that Naidānas based their interpretations on the primary cause of the visualisation of the Vedic verses whereas Aitihāsikas tried to interpret Vedic verses on the basis of the history of the origin of the Universe associated with them. Here the word history should not be confused with the human history, but the history of the origin of the Universe. Different Mantras were visualised keeping in view the various steps/phases of the origin of the Universe. So, Aitihāsikas made history of the various phases of the origin of the Universe as the basis of their interpretations, while Naidānas took the help of the primary cause of the visualisation of the Vedic Mantras for their interpretations.

It appears that a work entitled Nidāna, which embodied ancient legends explaining the primary cause of visualisation of Vedic verses, existed in the age of the Sūtras, because the *Bṛhaddevatā* (5,23) refers to such a work in the following verse after narrating the legend connected with the *RV.* (5.2), 'This couplet (5.2.29) is mentioned in the Brāhmaṇa of the Bhallavins; such is the Vedic passage cited in the work entitled Nidāna belonging to the Sāmavedins. It shows that the Sāmavedins had a work named Nidāna which contained legends relating to the visualisation of Vedic verses. This view is also corroborated by the following statement of the *Vāsıṣṭha Dharma-Sūtra* (I.14), 'Now the Bhāllavins also quote the (following) gāthā in the Nidāna.' Durgāchārya also lends his support to the view that a work entitled Nidāna existed in ancient times. So explaining the word Naidāna used in the *Nirukta* (7.12), Durgāchārya opines that those who know the work named Nidāna are called *Naidānāḥ*. It seems that the work Nidāna mentioned in ancient literature has been irretrievably lost. Therefore the Naidāna system of Vedic interpretation is known in name only, and we do not find any definite specimen of this system of interpretation

Aitihāsika School of Vedic Interpretation

The word Itihāsa has been used in the sense of the allegorical narratives depicting the history of creation. Aitihāsikas were those who used to interpret Vedic verses on the basis of the allegorical narratives underlying the various aspects of the history of creation. The Vedas deal with the knowledge of creation. Yajña depicts the process of creation and the tradition of the Itihāsa and Purāna depicted the history of creation by way of allegorical narratives. So the Vedas, as the knowledge of creation are intimately related to the history of creation and can be best explained and understood with the history of creation. That is why it has been repeatedly said:

इतिहासपुराणाभ्याम् वेदं समुपबृंहयेत्।

itihāsa purāṇābhyām vedaṁ samupabṛṁhyeta.

That is, the Vedic verses should be interpreted with

the help of Itihāsa and Purāṇa associated with them.

This school of Vedic interpretation survives by name only and it seems that it has been irretrievably lost. We have to satisfy ourselves only with stray references of it here and there in the Vedic literature. We come across in the Vedic and post-Vedic literature number of allegorical narratives depicting the historical aspects of various natural phenomenon forming the basis of Aitihāsika interpretation of certain hymns of the *Ṛgveda*. Among them, the narrative relating to Ocean churning, the war between Indra and Vṛtra, the war between devas and asuras, dialogue between Yama and Yamī, Narrative of Gotama and Ahilyā are prominent and well known.

The earliest specimens of the Aitihāsika interpretation of Vedic Mantras are met within the Brāhmaṇas. Several allegorical narratives concerning the Aitihāsika (historical) interpretation of the Vedic Mantras are in the Brāhmaṇa portion of the *Kṛṣṇa Yajurveda*, *Taittirīya Brāhmaṇa*, *Aitareya Brāhmaṇa*, *Jaiminīya Brāhmaṇa*, and *Panchviñśa Brāhmaṇa*. For instance, the Brāhmaṇa portion of the *Maitrāyaṇī Saṁhitā* contains the allegorical narratives relating to Urvaśī (lightening) and Purūravas (clouds) (1.6.12; 3.9.5); clipping of wings of parvatas (clouds) (1.10.13); Indra (electric force) and Triśirā Viśvarūpa (universe divided into three heads, i.e. Pṛthivī, Antarikṣa and Dyau) (2.4.1); Prajāpati (Milky way) and his daughters (27 constellations) (3.6.5; 4.2.12). The *Kṛṣṇa Yajurveda* Saṁhitā also mentions the allegorical narratives of Uravaśī-Purūravas (8.10), Indra-Viśvarūpa (12.10) etc. A plethora of examples can also be quoted from other extant and non-extant Brāhmaṇas.

Here it may not be out of context to point out that in the *Atharvaveda*, the *Sāṭyāyana Brāhmaṇa*, the *Gopatha Brāhmaṇa*, etc. the word Purāṇa occurs immediately after Itihāsa, e.g Itihāsa-purāṇam, Itihāsa-purāṇāni, etc. It shows that Itihāsa and Purāṇa are closely related to each other. That is why both these words are found coupled together in ancient works. The *Chhāndogya Upanıṣad* (7.1.2.4) declares the Itihāsa-Purāṇa to be the fifth Veda.

इतिहासपुराण: पंचमो वेदानां वेद: ।

Itihāsa purāṇaḥ pañchamo vedānāṁ vedaḥ.

If we go by the Śaṅkara's commentary on the *Bṛhdāraṇyaka Upanıṣad* (2.4.10), the Itihāsa is the description of the creation of the Universe and narration of events connected with various heavenly bodies is Purāṇa. The definition of Purāṇa has been given as under:

सर्गश्च प्रतिसर्गश्च वंशो मन्वन्तराणि च ।
वंशानुचरितं चैव पुराणपंच लक्षणम् ।।

sargaśca pratisargaśca vañśo manvantarāṇi ca
vañśānucharitaṁ chaiva purāṇa-pañchalakṣaṇam.

That is, creation, decreation, the lineage of heavenly bodies and chronology of various events in the history of the creation of the universe and description of the order of lineage of heavenly bodies is the subject matter of Purāṇas.

In nutshell, it can be said that Aitihāsikas (historical school of Vedic Interpretation) tried to add the historical context of the creation of the universe to the knowledge of creation contained in the Vedas.

Ancient and Medieval Commentators of the Vedas

In addition to the various schools of interpretations of the Vedas, we also meet with various ancient and mediaeval Bhāṣyakāras of the Vedas. A brief description of such interpreters is appended below for the knowledge of our readers.

1. **Skandaswāmī** (Kali 37th Century, i.e. c. 6th century A.D.)□ The ancient most commentary of the *Ṛgveda* available today is by Skanda Swāmī. He appears to be the most ancient commentator of the *Ṛgveda.* Skanda Swāmī's commentary enjoys great respect in the domain of Vedic exegesis. We are able to reflect some light on the parenthood and birthplace of Skanda Swāmī on the basis of some Ślokas appended by himself at the end of his commentary. For instance, there is a Śloka rendered at the end of the first Aṣṭaka of the *Ṛgveda-bhāṣya* which recalls Bhartṛdhruva as his father and Valabhī, the famous capital of Gujarat as his residential place. The Śloka reads as under:

वलभीविनिवास्येताम् ऋगर्थागम्सम्हृतिम् ।

भर्तृध्रुव सुतश्चक्रे स्कन्धस्वामी यथा स्मृति ।।

Valabhīvinivāsyetām ṛgarthāgamsaṁhṛtim.
bhartṛdhruva sutaścakre skandasvāmī yathā smṛti.

Skand Swāmī was the teacher of Hari Swāmī the esteemed commentator of the *Śatapatha Brāhmaṇa.* This fact has been disclosed by Hari Swāmī himself in one of the introductory verses of the *Śatapatha Bhāṣya* as under:

व्याख्याकृत्वाऽध्यापयन्मां श्री स्कन्धस्वामी मे गुरुः ।

vyākhyā kṛtvā'dhyāpayanmāṁ śrī skandsvāmyasti me guruḥ. (Verse -7)

Hari Swāmī gives the time-period of his Bhāṣya as

3040th year of the Kali era as under:

यदाब्दानां कलेर्जग्मुः त्रिंशत् शतानि वै।
चतुर्विंशत् समाश्चान्यास्तदा भाष्यमिदं कृतम्।।

yadābdānāṁ kalerjagmuḥ sapta triṁśatśatāni vai
catvāriṁśatsamāscānyāstadā bhāṣyamıdaṁ kṛtam.

'After passing 3040 years of the Kali era, this Bhāṣ ya is composed.'

This puts Hari Swāmī around 62 BC. If Skandasvāmī is taken as the teacher of Harisvāmī, his time period goes around 100 BC. Thus Skand Swāmī can be said as contemporary of Kālidāsa of Jyotirvidābharaṇa and Vikramaditya II.

Skand Swāmī has rendered his valuable commentary on Yāska's *Nirukta* Yāska (Kali era 2000-2100 or c 10th-11th century BC).

Skand Swāmī (100 BC) has rendered a significant but brief commentary on the *Ṛgveda* which runs till the fourth Aṣṭaka of the *Ṛgveda.* Sāyaṇa (Kali 4416-4488, i.e. c. 1314-1386 AD) owes a lot to him, this is proved beyond any shadow of a doubt.

2. **Nārāyaṇa** (Kali 30th century, i.e. 1st century BC): Nārāyaṇa is the next commentator of the *Ṛgveda* in order. He was either contemporary to Skand Swāmī or his successor. This is proved by the statement of Veṅkaṭamādhava made by him during the course of his *Ṛgbhāṣya.* He comments as follows:

स्कन्दस्वामी नारायण उद्गीथ इति ते क्रमात् चक्रुः।
सहैकमृग्भाष्यं पदवाक्यार्थगोचरम्।।

Skandaswāmī nārāyaṇa udgītha iti te kramāt cakruḥ
sahaikamṛgbhāṣyaṁ padavākyārthagocaram

'Skandasvāmī, Nārāyaṇa, and Udgītha wrote only one commentary on *Ṛgveda* in order of sequence.

From the aforementioned statement, one can easily

confer that Skand Swāmī, Nārāyaṇa and Udgītha didn't compose their separate commentaries on the *Ṛgveda*, but they made it their joint venture attempting separately on the beginning, middle and last portions of the *Ṛgveda.* Thus the Skand Swāmī attempted his comments on the first portion of the *RV.* i.e. from the 1st Aṣṭaka to the 4th Aṣṭaka and Nārāyaṇa must have handled the middle portion and Udgītha the last one. Today, we have not yet come across the said commentary of Nārāyaṇa on the middle portion of the *RV.*

3. **Udgītha** (Kali 30th century,i.e. c. 1st century BC): Udgītha is the third commentator of the *RV.* He may also be considered as the colleague of Skandswāmī in his venture. He also stands either contemporary or successor of Skanda and Nārāyaṇa. His commentary is available on the last portion of the *RV.* At the end of each *Adhyāya* he introduces himself as:

वनवासी विनिर्गताचार्यस्य उद्‌गीथस्य कृता ऋग्भाष्ये।

vanavāsī vinirgatācāryasya udgīthasya kṛtā ṛgbhāṣye.

It is quite obvious from the above statement that he migrated from the Vanavāsī region and his association with Skand Swāmī of Gujarat also tells about his place of migration as Valabhī. In ancient times the western part of modern Karnataka was famous as Vanavāsī region. Thus Karnataka may be taken as the original place of Udgītha.

Sāyaṇa (Kali 4416-4488, i.e. c. 1314-1386 AD) and Ātmānanda (Kali 45th century,i.e. c. 13th century) have quoted Udgītha in their commentaries. Udgītha followed the pattern of Skandswāmī. Sāyaṇa also owes Udgītha for his commentary on the *RV.*

4. **Mādhava Bhaṭṭa**: Mādhava Bhaṭṭa is also one of the ancient commentators whose whereabouts are unknown. His gloss on the first Aṣṭaka is available today which is published from Madras University.

5. **Veṅkaṭa Mādhava**: Veṅkaṭamādhava wrote his

commentary on the full text of the *RV.* From the colophon of his *Ṛgbhāṣya* we come to know that his grandfather's name was Mādhava, his father's name was Vaṅkaṭācārya, his grandmother's name was Bhavagola and his mother's name was Sundarī. His maternal surname was Vasiṣṭha and the paternal surname was Kauśika. He had a younger brother, too, named as Saṅkarṣaṇa. He had two sons, *viz.*, Veṅkaṭa and Govinda. He came from Chola country or modern Andhra Pradesh. (Cf. *Ṛgbhāṣya*, Anantaśayana book series, Intr. PP. 7-8.)

Sāyaṇa quotes the views of Mādhava Bhaṭṭa in his commentary on the *RV.* 10.86.1 which conforms to the commentary of Veṅkaṭa Mādhava. Thus it can easily be inferred that Veṅkaṭa Mādhava proceeds Sāyaṇa.

Veṅkaṭa Mādhava was well versed in Brāhmaṇas. He attached great significance to the Brāhmaṇas for the interpretation of the Vedas than to the Grammar and the *Nirukta.* According to him, the unknown and doubtful meanings of the Mantras can be ascertained well at the hands of the scholars well versed in the Brāhmaṇas. Modern scholars whose study is confined only to the *Nirukta* and grammar are able to understand only the quarter part of the Saṁhitā, but the scholars excelled in the Brāhmaṇas know the diction of words and are able to speak of the complete meaning of the Saṁhitā, e.g.

अस्माभिस्त्विह मन्त्राणामर्थः प्रत्येकमुच्यते।
येऽज्ञाता ये च सन्दिग्धास्तेषां वृद्धेषु निर्णयः।।

संहितायास्तुरीयांसं विजानन्त्यधुनातानाः।
निरुक्तव्याकरणयोरासीत् येषां परिश्रमः।

अथ ये ब्राह्मणार्थानां विवेक्तारः कृतश्रमाः।।
शब्द रीतिं विजानन्ति ते सर्वं कथ्यन्त्यपि।

asmābhistviha mantrāṇāmarthaḥ pratyekamucyate
ye'jñātā ye ca sandigdhāsteṣāṁ vṛddheṣu nirṇaya

saṁhitāyāsturīyāṁsaṁ vijānantyadhunātanāḥ
niruktavyākaraṇyorāsīt yeṣāṁ pariśramaḥ

atha ye brāhmaṇarthānāṁ vivektāraḥ kṛtaśramāḥ
śabdarītiṁ vijānanti te sarvaṁ kathyantyapi.

In fact, Brāhmaṇika tradition was the actual inheritor of the original Vedārtha. That is why Veṅkaṭa Mādhava laid the maximum stress on the need of Brāhmaṇas for the interpretation of the Vedas. In his own commentary, which is conspicuous with the principle of brevity, he avoids the references to grammar as it was done later by Sāyaṇa and others.

6. **Dhānuṣka Yajvā**: Dhānuṣka Yajvā has also been referred to as the commentator of three the Vedas by Vedācārya in his *Sudarśana-mīmāṁsā.* He was a Vaiṣṇava Ācārya. Nothing except this is known either about him or his commentary.

7. **Ānanda Tīrtha** (Kali 45th century,i.e. c. 13th century): Ānanda Tīrtha was famous by the name of Mādhava. He was the Vaiṣṇava saint who propagated the Dvaitavāda. He wrote his commentary on the 40 Sūktas of the first Maṇḍala of the *RV.* Nārāyaṇa is the theme of his commentary because in the *Gītā* it has been declared that all the Vedas speak about Me (Nārāyaṇa).

वेदैश्च सर्वैरहमेव वेद्यः

Vedaiśca sarvairahmeva ved'yaḥ

Mādhava declares himself at the beginning of his commentary

स पुराणत्वात् पुमान् नाम पुरुषे सूक्त ईरितः।
स एवाखिल वेदार्थः सर्व शास्त्रार्थ एव च।।

sa pūrṇatvāt pumān nāma pauruṣe sūkta īritaḥ
sa evākhila vedārthaḥ sarvaśāstrārtha eva ca.

'Nārāyaṇa, being All perfect, has been called as Puruṣa in the Puruṣa Sūkta. So, the same has been subjected to all the Vedas and Śāstras.'

He lived between c1139 AD and c1278 AD.

8. **Ātmānanda** (Kali 45th century, i.e. 13th century AD): Ātmānanda rendered his commentary on the Asyavāmīya Sūkta. He refers to Skanda, Bhāskara etc., but Sāyaṇa doesn't find his mention in his commentary. Hence he has been considered to be the predecessor of Sāyaṇa. He can also be placed somewhere in the 13th century AD. His commentary is based on *Viṣṇudharmottara*. According to him, Skand's commentary pertains to rituals or Yajñas. The *Nirukta* deals with the astronomical sense. But his commentary deals with the spiritual sense.

9. **Sāyaṇa** (Kali 4416-4488, i.e. c.1314-1386 AD): Sāyaṇa is one of the prominent and last among the ancient commentators. His commentaries on the Vedas and allied literature are very famous. In fact, Sāyaṇa is known by the Vedas and the Vedas are known by Sāyaṇa. Sāyaṇa composed the ritualistic interpretation of the Vedas.

He was the minister of Bukk Rai who was the founder of Vijayanagar. For 16 years, he held the charge of Prime ministership of Bukka Rai. He mostly belongs to the period of 2nd half of the 45th century of Kaliyuga, i.e. 14th century AD. He was the younger brother of Mādhava. In fact, Sāyaṇa's commentary acts as the lighthouse for the interpretation of the Vedas. No interpretation of the Vedas is possible without Sāyaṇa. All the later commentators dwelt heavily upon Sāyaṇa while rendering their commentaries.

Modern Eastern and Western Interpreters of the Vedas

The contribution of Western scholars to the field of Vedic exegesis is no less remarkable whatsoever be the quality of their work. So far as the translation of the *RV.* is concerned Dr. H.H. Wilson rendered the translation of the entire *RV.* following Sāyaṇa's Bhāṣya in 1850. Secondly, H. Grassmann in 1876-1877 attempted a poetical translation of the *RV.* In German language following Roth's philological method. Ludwig also rendered his translation of the *RV.* running into 6 volumes between 1876 and 1888. Apart from the above-mentioned translations, we meet with Griffith's poetical translation. It was published in 1889-92 from Kāśi. This translation is also based upon Sāyaṇa. A German scholar H. Oldenberg (1824-1920) also published his translation of the *RV.* from Berlin in two volumes in 1909-1912. This translation is also very thought-provoking and may be called as critical one so far as the references of other translators on each and every hymn are concerned. This is all about what the occidental scholars did.

Here in India we also come across with Swami Dayanand Saraswati (1824-1883) who attempted Bhāṣya on the *Ṛgveda* till 7th maṇḍala and 61 Sūktas and the complete *Yajurveda.* Though Swami Dayanand couldn't complete his Bhāṣya on the *Ṛgveda,* yet it has a great significance in the field of Vedic exegesis. If the literal translation of the Vedas is not possible without Sāyaṇa the actual translation of the Vedas cannot be rendered without the help of Dayanand. In his essay titled '*Dayanand and the Veda*', Sri Aurobindo comments as under:

> "Whatever may be the final and complete interpretation of the Vedas, Dayanand will be honoured as the first discoverer of the right clues. He has found out the keys of the doors that time had

closed and rent asunder the seals of the imprisoned fountains."

Swami Dayanand, in fact, was a living embodiment of Vedic life and thought. He marshalled the Vedas, Brāhmaṇas, Upavedas, and other Vedāṅgas. Moreover, he was not led by any preconceived notions and hence didn't try to project his own meanings upon the Vedas. He basically followed the traditional view registered in the Vedas and other allied literature. He also tried to interpret the Vedas on the basis of their internal evidence. According to him, the Vedas are Homo Mensura i.e. *Svataḥ Pramāṇa* and the authority of the Vedas cannot be challenged on the basis of other works since the Vedas are the books first ever produced by humanity in the library of the world. So far as the rich cultural and scientific background, within which the Vedas were composed, remains un-construed, no factual interpretation of the Vedas is possible.

To sum up it can be said that only two Bhāṣyas dominate the domain of Vedic exegesis, one by Sāyaṇa and the other by Swami Dayanand Saraswati.

References

Ahmed, Enayat (1993): Physical Geography, Kalyani Publisher, Delhi

Avadha Behari Tripathi (1968): *Bṛhat Saṁhitā* of Varāhamihira, Varanasi.

Bellikoth Rama: *Jaiminīya Upaniṣad Brāhmana,* K.

Bhagavaddatta (1920): *Ṛgveda par Vyākhyā,* Dayānanda College, Lahore.

Brahmadatta Jijñāsu: *Dayananda's Yājuṣa Bhāṣya Vivaraṇa.*

Brahma Muni Parivrājaka (1996): *Nirukta Sammarśah,* Sanskrit Tr. of *Nirukta,* Ajmer.

Dayananda Saraswati: *Yajurveda Bhāṣya,* Ajmer.

Dayananda Saraswati: *Ṛgbhāṣya,* Ajmer.

Dayananda Saraswati (1984): *Ṛgvedādibhāṣvabhūmikū,* de-Yudhisthira Mimansaka, Bahalgarh, Sonepat.

Eggeling, J.: *Śatapatha Brāhmaṇa,* Oxford, Clarenden Press.

Griffith R.T.H. (1957): *Text of White Yajurveda,* Varanasi, E.J. Lazarus.

Jwāla Prasad Miśra (1969): *Vājasaneyī Saṁhitā,* Bombay.

Kaegi, A.(1886): *Ṛgveda* Eng. Tr. Boston, Gim.

Kashinatha Shastri (1977): *Aitreya Brāhmana* with Sāyaṇa -Bhaṣya, Poona.

Keith, A.B. (1971): *Ṛgveda Brāhmaṇas, Aitareya* and *Kauṣ itaki Brāhmaṇas of Ṛgveda,* Delhi, Motilal.

Kṣemakaraṇa Trivedi (1920): *Gopatha Brāhmaṇa,* Prayāga.

Macdonell, A.A. (1904): *Bṛhaddevatā,* Harward Oriental Series.

Macdonell, A.A. (1963): *Vedic Mythology,* Varanasi Indological Book House.

Mahavir Sastrin (1908-21): *Taittirīya Brāhmaṇa* with the commentary of Bhaṭṭabhāskara Miśra, Mysore.

Max Müller, F. (1956): *Vedas,* Calcutta, Sushil Gupta.

Max Müller, F.: *Vedic Hymns,* Motilal, Delhi.

Motilal Sharma: *Śatpatha Brāhmaṇa, Vijñāna Bhāṣya,* Jaipur.

Oldenberg, H. (1886): *Sāṅkhāyana Gṛhya Sūtra,* Oxford.

Pandit, M.P. (1963): *Gems from the Vedas,* Ganesh.

Raghunandan Sharma (2016): *Vedic Sampatti,* Bombay, 2016.

Raghvir (1936): *Atharvaveda,* S. V. Granthamāla, Lohore.

Raghvir, Lokesh Chandra (1995): *Jaiminīya Brāhmaṇa,* SVS Nagpur.

Ram Kumar Rai: *Śaunakīya Bṛhaddevatā,* Varanasi.

Ravi Prakash Arya (1991): *Researches into Vedic and Linguistic Studies,* Indian Foundation for Vedic Science, Delhi.

Ravi Prakash Arya (1995): *Vedic Meteorology,* Indian Foundation for Vedic Science, Delhi.

Ravi Prakash Arya (2007): *Vedic and Classical Sanskrit,* Indian Foundation for Vedic Science, Delhi.

Ravi Prakash Arya (1996): *Ṛgveda Saṁhitā,* Primal Publications, Delhi.

Ravi Prakash Arya (1996/2): *Yajurveda Saṁhitā,* Indian Foundation for Vedic Science, Delhi.

Ravi Prakash Arya (1997): *Sāmaveda Saṁhitā,* Indian Foundation for Vedic Science, Delhi.

Samarpaṇānanda : *Śatapatha Brāhmaṇa* Sāmarpaṇa Bhāṣya. Prabhat Ashram Meerut.

Swami Shridhara Shastrin (1922): *Śāṅkhāyana Araṇyaka,* Anandashram, Poona.

Shripada Sharma (1942): *Kaṭha Saṁhitā,* Aundh.

Shripada Sharma (1943): *Kāṭhaka Saṁhitā,* Aundh.

Shripada Sharma (1943/2): *Maitrāyaṇī Saṁhitā,* Aundh.

Shripada Sharma (1943/3): *Maitrāyaṇī Saṁhitā* (Brāhmaṇa-portion), Aundh.

Shripada Sharma (1945): *Taittirīya Saṁhitā,* Aundh.

Uvaṭa & Mahidhara: *Vājasaneyī Saṁhitā,* Varanasi.

Vedapala Sunitha (1991-92): *Śatapatha ke Daśapatha, Part I & II,* Tilauradham, Rajasthan.

Vedapala Sunitha (1991): *Darśapūrnamāseṣṭirahasya Prakāśa,* Tilaura, Rajasthan.

Vishva Bandhu: *Ṛgveda-Skand, Udgitha, Veṅkaṭamādhava Kṛtā Vyākhyā Sahitā,* Hoshiarpur, Punjab.

Vishva Bandhu: *Vedic Word Concordance,* Lahore.

www.ingramcontent.com/pod-product-compliance
Lightning Source LLC
Chambersburg PA
CBHW031320040426
42443CB00005B/152
9788187710417